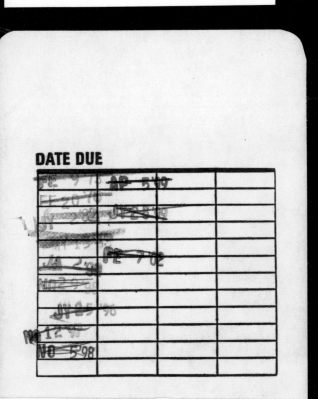

The Off-Broadway Experience

The OFF-

Prentice-Hall, Inc., Englewood Cliffs, N. J.

BROADWAY
Experience

BY HOWARD GREENBERGER

To K.S.L. Brownlie . . . for believing

How did she help me?
Let me count the ways:
Creatively, functionally
(with an assist from Joan and Joel Pecoraro),
editorially, spiritually—enormously!*

*Francine Forest

CON

TENTS

The Off-Broadway Experience

I
OB's Bio

LEE SIMONSON

A young artist, whose achievements in scene-painting have already had a far-reaching effect on the American stage. Has shown much daring in color and lighting

ROBERT STRANGE

Who has appeared in all of the Washington Square bills, notwithstanding the fact that he has remained actively engaged in business; an actor with authority and exceptional talent

WILLIAM PENNINGTON

Perhaps his most valuable contribution to the success of the Players has been his unerring and poetic flair for stage lighting, and for beautiful color effects in general

FLORENCE ENRIGHT

...done a little amateur acting ...roducing, before joining the ...s: has appeared in their ... bill. Her greatest successes ... been in very youthful rôles

HELEN WESTLEY

Was once a professional actress Retired and joined the ranks of the Players. Has a wide artistic range and has appeared in all of the Players' bills since their beginning

EDWARD GOODMAN

Director of the Washington Square Players and the moving spirit in their so creditable enterprise. A New Yorker, born and bred. Always interested in the theatre. Besides directing the artistic destinies of the Players, he has produced, and written, some of their successful plays

PHILIP MOELLER

...e of the founders of the Players. ...s produced and directed many of ...ir plays. Author of several of their ...hter and most popular comedies

HOLLAND HUDSON

The competent business manager of the Washington Square Players. Has helped to keep the company on a sane and well-ordered financial footing

JOSEPHINE MEYER

... Washington Square Players' ... play reader. An author and ...strator on her own account. A ...ic and reader of the first ability

RALPH ROEDER

A sensitive and appealing actor of the deepest cultivation. Has translated many Italian, French, and German plays for his fellow Players

SPALDING HALL

The painter and artist at the head of the Players' modernist-school costume department. Has also acted with ability in many of their plays

LUCY HUFFAKER

The tireless and efficient manager of the Players' press department, and always a hostess unto herself "out front"—evenings and matinees

The Washington Square Players

A dozen of the able young men and women who have contributed to the success of what is now generally conceded to be our most important theatrical experiment of recent years

The old man trusts wholly to slow contrivance and gradual progression; the youth expects to force his way by genius, vigor and precipitance. The old man pays regard to riches, and the youth reverences virtue. . . . Age looks with anger on the temerity of youth, and youth with contempt on the scrupulosity of age. SAMUEL JOHNSON

OFF BROADWAY was conceived out of necessity. Playwrights, directors, producers, actors, composers, and designers of costumes, sets, and lighting had to have room to stretch the legitimate theater's artistic limits, so long constricted by the market operations of Broadway. In this account of how creative talents made a haven for working toward rewards other than monetary, Off Broadway will be referred to as OB—the opposite of the theater of BO (Box Office).

At the turn of the century, when OB was born, the behind-the-scenes picture of the stage was not as pretty as the romantic fare presented before the footlights. The businessmen, who called themselves producers, were tired of sharing their profits from road tours with local theater owners. To keep all the returns for themselves, the Shuberts, and Klaw and Erlanger formed theatrical syndicates by buying up most of the houses throughout the country for their own touring production. This virtual monopoly continued until the motion-picture giants moved in during the twenties.

Until the movie take-over, the big theatrical merchants had the more venturesome producers at their mercy, and the old-time stock companies all but disappeared. The situation was as melodramatic as the plays of that era. That a Mansfield, a Mrs. Fiske, a Belasco, a Fitch, or a Moody could have emerged meant either that virtue triumphed or that they were in collusion.

Such strangleholds also gripped Europe and caused a revolt against the prevalent uncreative system. The result was the "art" theaters, Dublin's Abbey, the Moscow Art Players, London's Independent Theatre, the Théâtre Libre de Paris, and their like that helped develop the great turn-of-the-century playwrights: Shaw, Synge, O'Casey, Ibsen, Chekhov, and Strindberg. And so, like the catharsis of tragedy itself, from evil came good.

In America, this reawakening to theater as art was initially cultivated in universities. From there and from Europe the new theatrical awareness spread to socially conscious people, whose frustration with existing theater was one more manifestation of their dissatisfaction with general conditions of the day, and led to the creation of OB in 1905.

The first sounds OB made were pleas for social reforms. The grumblings were voiced in free radical plays produced by Julius Hopp at the Progressive Stage Society in New York City and later presented at the Wage Earners' Theatre, the Education Theatre for Schools, and the Theatre League. OB did not come into its own, however, until the beginning of the next decade.

For want of a fuller artistic experience, some Greenwich Village intellectuals formed such organizations as the Socialist Press Club and the Arts Club, which used to meet in members' homes to read plays that were not being done because the stage was a commercial enterprise. One such group of devotees, the Liberal Club, decided to move from just appreciating to actually presenting important, unproduced plays. This resolution was made at the Boni Brothers' bookshop on Washington Square, where they gathered regularly, inspiring their name—the Washington Square Players.

The company's plan, which remained almost intact when it eventually evolved into the Theatre Guild many years later, was to produce new American and European plays of "artistic merit" in direct competition to Broadway. To make this "uplift" available to as many people as possible, the price of admission was set at fifty cents. Funds came from public subscription and from members of the organization itself: Lawrence Langner, a patent attorney who also wrote plays; Theresa Helburn, Edward Goodman, and Philip Moeller, potential playwrights; Lee Simonson, editor of *Creative Arts;* Louis Untermeyer, a poetry lover; and Walter Lippman, a columnist. With only a few hundred dollars and a handful of subscribers, these theater-loving novices put their ideals into action at the tiny Bandbox Theatre at 57th Street and Third Avenue.

The officially recognized debut of OB was on February 19, 1915. That was the night the Players opened with three one-act plays by Langner, Goodman, and Maurice Maeterlinck, plus a pantomime, all performed rather amateurishly. They intended to give only Friday and Saturday night performances, but, to their surprise, the second night was sold out, so they had to add a third evening. By the end of the season, the Players went through four programs of one-acters. The short-play form became typical of small theaters, because it allows the greatest freedom for experimentation at the least expense, and it is easier for beginners to cope with than the complexities of a full-length script.

As was almost always to be true throughout the days of OB, revenue was never quite enough to meet costs, which seemed to be ever rising. Yet that did not stop the Players. This brave band, after a couple of years, set out to try Broadway, and moved to the Comedy Theatre on West 41st Street. Their annual rent there was $32,000, which was four times as much as they were paying at their previous home. Professional actors were employed, and as much as $15,000 was spent on mounting a production. Of course, ticket prices had to go up. Many of their initial supporters felt that the wider scope they attained on Broadway hardly compensated for the loss of their original ambience. They were done in, however, by the greatest drama the world had yet seen when key members of the Players went off for service in World War I.

The final bill of the Washington Square Players, staged on May 13, 1918, included, prophetically enough, Susan Glaspell's *Close the Book*. Their four-year history is filled with important achievements: the presentation of sixty-two one-act plays and pantomimes as well as six long dramas; the training of Katharine Cornell, Roland Young, and Frank Conroy; the emergence of Edward Goodman and Philip Moeller as directors; and the chance provided Lee Simonson to design sets. The enduring monument of the Washington Square Players came from their reorganization after World War I into Broadway's Theatre Guild.

With the prestige of nearly fifty years of success on the Main Stem the Theatre Guild returned to OB in 1964, only to fail with Paul Shyre's adaptation of John Hersey's novel, *The Child Buyer*, and with another production that closed immediately after opening night, *All Women Are One*. Proof again of the old show business adage: No one, no matter how wise or important, knows what makes theatrical success.

Long before that, when the Washington Square Players were just beginning, their decision not to produce a certain play resulted in the start of their chief competition, OB's second most famous theater, the Provincetown Players. Susan Glaspell and her husband, George Cram Cook, were originally involved with the Washington Square Players until that group rejected the couple's *Suppressed Desires* as too strange. This made the authors decide to try it out on their own.

In the summer of 1915, several Greenwich Village artists and writers who were vacationing in Provincetown on Cape Cod were invited to the home of Hutchins Hapgood for a performance of the almost stifled *Suppressed Desires* and a play written by Hapgood's wife, *Constancy*. Encouraged by the response of their guests, the Cooks and Hapgoods took over an old fish house at the end of a wharf, converted it into a theater, and gave it the likeliest name: the Wharf Theatre.

The next summer, Eugene O'Neill came to this spawn

hatcher of talent. He brought with him *Bound East for Cardiff*, a play that no one had appreciated—not even his drama teacher at Yale, Professor George Baker—until it was read to an assemblage at Cook's home. From there to the stage of the Wharf was a matter of weeks, and it was only a few more months before this first play of O'Neill's premiered in New York.

Putting up the set for *Bound East for Cardiff* at the Playwrights' Theater, 1916. O'Neill on ladder; Hippolyte Havel, seated; William (Scotty) Stuart in overalls; Jig Cook, holding pole (Paul Thompson Photograph by permission of Arthur and Barbara Gelb, authors of *O'Neill*, Harper & Row)

In autumn, the Wharf Theatre people moved back to the Village to set up shop at 139 MacDougal Street. Five hundred subscribers enrolled at five dollars apiece for the season. Dues were charged, because the Provincetowners had to be run as a private club in order to avoid falling under the jurisdiction of stringent city building ordinances. Sad to say, fifty years later, those who wished to make similar cultural contributions to the community at the Caffè Cino and at the Café La Mama also were harried because they were unable to meet the requirements of such antiquated laws.

Despite the fact that unprofessionalism was preferred by the Provincetowners, since they felt it gave them a sense of freedom from convention, the critics perceived their promise. After nine bills, it was time to return to Provincetown for summer replenishment. The following fall, the beginning of World War I had a chaotic effect not only on what they presented, but also on the organization itself.

Rescued from artistic and financial difficulties by the strong will of Mary Eleanor Fitzgerald, "Fitzi," the Provincetowners moved to a new home at 133 MacDougal Street. This was where, in 1920, the increasingly esteemed O'Neill decided to put on his most ambitious play till then, *The Emperor Jones*.

That production proved to be their greatest success, as well as the cause of their downfall. The reviews were so ecstatic that their subscription list jumped to 1,500 almost immediately, and it was decided that the show should be taken uptown. Working in two areas dissipated their energies, and the Provincetown Players lasted only a few more years. Soon afterward, O'Neill took over the helm and organized the Provincetown Playhouse and The Greenwich Village Theatre to present plays of his own creation, and those of others in whom he believed. An audience could not be found for their worthy productions. After a few seasons, they were almost bankrupt but managed to raise $1,500 to put on *In Abra-*

ham's Bosom, The Biography of a Negro in Seven Scenes by
Paul Green, and it won the 1927 Pulitzer Prize. When even
this didn't help, the discouraged O'Neill decided to give up
producing and devote himself completely to his writing.
O'Neill brought OB into prominence, and twenty years later
OB reciprocated by restoring his fading glory.

The only existing souvenir of the old days is the Neighborhood Playhouse. It has survived as a school, but it began in
1907 as a major artistic influence on the teeming East Side. To
feed the hunger of immigrants for theater, the Henry Street
Settlement House presented festivals and pantomimes. A
dramatic club emerged out of this which attracted two prominent patrons of the arts, Alice and Irene Lewisohn. In the
winter of 1915, these benefactresses gave this amateur company its own theater at 466 Grand Street. From these beginnings came a world-renowned troupe that was hailed for its
exquisite productions of exotic plays, such as *The Dybbuk* and
The Little Clay Cart, as well as Chinese drama, and Italian
Commedia del' Arte. The admission price? From ten to fifty
cents.

For the Neighborhood Playhouse, too, the bright vision
had to fade before cold fact. In 1927, when the Lewisohn sisters no longer underwrote its annual deficit of $40,000, the
theater operation ceased. Just one of the Neighborhood Playhouse's original functions, that of training people for theater,
has remained.

Those were the three most famous companies of early OB,
but there were others: the Bramhall Theatre, the Brooklyn
Repertory, and the Negro Players, who were the first to give
blacks a chance to be in plays about their own people, the
Cherry Lane Theatre, and the East and West Players with
their Yiddish productions. All these and more played a vital
part in the advancement of theater in the twenties.

The 1929 stock-market crash sent OB into a decline. Backers became scarce. For a great part of the audience even a

half-dollar admission was too much, especially since escape could be had at movie theaters showing double features with dishes and Bingo thrown in for just fifteen cents. The only theatrical light to shine with OB brilliance during the dark times of the early thirties was Eva LeGallienne's Civic Repertory Theatre on 14th Street. Though this organization was recruited from uptown, at heart it was really OB, because its home was off the beaten path, its prices were low, and its motives were thoroughly artistic.

Twenty-five classics were presented in repertory, with stars like Alla Nazimova and Joseph Schildkraut. Even with that appealing combination, financial ruin was a constant threat, and finally the production of *Alice in Wonderland* put Miss LeGallienne into a real hole. This show was so extravagant that it had to be moved to Broadway to try to make it pay for itself. When this did not work, the company disappeared into the hinterlands for fifteen years. Then in 1947, when Miss LeGallienne again returned to Broadway with *Alice*, this time in repertory with other plays, she was forced to realize that the Main Stem is no place for such noble ambitions.

Once more, the need for social reform, which had given OB its start, began to be expressed in theatrical terms, instigating OB's resurgence during the Depression. Leading the way was the Theatre Union with *Stevedore,* and *Waiting for Lefty,* the play that made Clifford Odets the dramatic spokesman of the unrest of his time. His liberal plays found their main outlet in the Group Theatre, which, though on Broadway, had all the unbridled spirit of OB's adherents. This was not surprising since many of its members came from the Theatre Guild, née the Washington Square Players. The Group explored techniques of performance based on the Stanislavsky concepts pioneered by the Moscow Art Theatre and interpreted by Lee Strasberg and Harold Clurman. The realism that was brought to the American stage expressed the striving of the thirties for greater humanitarianism.

The trials of the working classes were delineated by the Worker's Drama League, the Artef, the Jewish Workers Theatre, the Ukrainian Dramatic Circle, the Worker's Laboratory Theatre, and the Theatre Collective. And when the cares of garment workers were clothed in the song and satire of *Pins and Needles*, a revue by Harold Rome, produced by members of the International Ladies' Garment Workers' Union, the public showed interest in their plight.

Paying jobs for theater people were so scarce that the government, for the first time, stepped in to help the arts by setting up the nationwide Federal Theatre; six theaters were allocated to various sections of New York under the Works Progress Administration—one was run by Orson Welles and became the basis for the Mercury Theatre. There was tremendous variety in the hundreds of shows that were presented, but its most original contribution was lively re-creations of events of the day called *The Living Newspaper*. The Federal Theatre got into trouble because it was considered radical, and after four years Congress did away with its appropriation.

"Agit-prop" dramas flowed from other sources. This use of theater to create agitation and disseminate propaganda made the stage an active power in the fight against social problems. In the forefront, tending toward the left, were the Theatre of Action and the New Theatre League alerting the people against the encroaching horrors of fascism and war.

When World War II came, the public only wanted escape and dramas of heroism. Originality had to be content with a single OB outlet: the Experimental Theatre, sponsored by the Dramatists' Guild and Actors' Equity, which kept the hope for the future of the theater alive by staging avant-garde plays, and by giving awards and scholarships to their creators.

The greatest phase for OB began almost immediately after the war. To remedy the lack of opportunity in the established theater, returning veterans took matters into their own hands and set up nearly three hundred theaters within three years. And so began—after nearly fifty years of being looked upon as small-time theater—OB's Golden Era, the period when the designation "off Broadway" was originated as an expression of respect for a distinguished and distinctive cultural entity that was no longer to be measured against the commercial colossus.

During the fifties, OB reached maturity. The increasing extravagance of Broadway fostered the growth of OB. Few producers could afford to try the new and unknown or the old and special which would have no attraction for the expense-account set that had developed during the war and made going to hit entertainments a symbol of prestige.

Those who really loved the theater for its own sake were mostly young intellectuals who could not compete for spiraling-priced tickets, especially when the cost was added to the other expenses of an evening out—baby-sitter, dinner, and drinks. Broadway's declining level of content also disturbed these aware enthusiasts. To get the kind of theatrical stimulation they wanted at a price they could afford, they had to walk down alleys other than Shubert, and wherever they turned—away from Broadway—what they were looking for was there. All over town actors, directors, and playwrights were making theaters out of any available shelter that could house a provocative production. And this selective audience came because to them theatergoing was a way of life, not a *nouveau-riche* event booked by a scalper or a theater-party lady and used to gauge one's social-financial position—the more expensive and difficult to get the ticket was (and still is today) the better, making the balcony a virtual ghetto.

The front-running and longer-lasting organizations in the postwar OB movement were the Associated Playwrights, Inc., the New Stages, the Playcrafters, Onstage, and Originals Only. The attention they attracted made others realize that here was a way of meeting the ever-present problem facing most people in the theater—to have somewhere to work for immediate satisfaction and future recognition. These self-made opportunities gave young aspirants, if not food to eat, at least a pillow for dreams.

Actors' Equity gave OB official recognition in 1950 by setting union regulations for 199- and 299-seat theaters outside the area bound by Fifth and Ninth avenues, from 34th to 56th streets in the city of New York. The minimum salary was five dollars a week; today that figure is about one hundred dollars on a sliding scale. The original stipend may seem only a token payment, but it did mean that OB's efforts were at last considered professional. That lift in status also pushed up overhead, because other unions followed suit.

Though production expenses were comparatively minimal then, few chances were taken on original scripts—especially since showcasing actors was one of its original objectives. OB found stability in specializing in the presentation of Broadway failures with *succès di estime* reputations, classics with a built-in following, and imports with a presold curiosity value. No excuses need be made, however, when the public could see and actors could appear in quality productions of important plays. Representative of the best of the multitude of such offerings were Paul Shyre's O'Casey series, Chekhov as done by David Ross, Shakespeare interpreted by Joseph Papp, and the plays rescued from the library by the Phoenix Theatre—just an indication of the many superior works OB made available. And who in America would have experienced the wonders of Beckett, Ionesco, and Genêt but for OB?

It was not until nearly the end of the Golden Era that a major new American playwright proved himself on OB's grounds. Edward Albee made it with a one-act play, *The Zoo Story*. It was on a double bill with *Krapp's Last Tape*, directed by Alan Schneider who staged most of Beckett and was soon to do the same for Albee. After Albee's success, he and his coproducers, Richard Barr and Clinton Wilder, set up a playwright's workshop to unearth new authors. The results have been only promising, but one blockbuster did emerge, Mart Crowley's *The Boys in the Band*.

Despite the controversy over whether or not its obligation to do a greater number of worthwhile original scripts—if more actually existed—was fulfilled, OB need not make any excuses. More attention was paid the new playwrights of the fifties and early sixties OB than anywhere else in the world. Numberless and nameless writers and plays were introduced for every one who attained some measure of recognition. Those hailed were: Leslie Stevens' *Bullfight*, Arnold Weinstein's *The Red Eye of Love*, Jack Richardson's *The Prodigal*, James Lee's *Career*, Rick Besoyan's *Little Mary Sunshine*, Frank D. Gilroy's *Who'll Save the Ploughboy?*, Murray Schisgal's *The Typist* and *The Tiger*, LeRoi Jones' *The Dutchman*, and William Hanley's *Mrs. Dally Has A Lover*. Many of these playwrights have already surpassed their initial achievements. As for the others, only time will tell what their ultimate contributions will be, but OB got them onstage, and now everyone is waiting for encores.

The only company to have a continuity of production since the fifties is the Circle in the Square of Leigh Connell, Theodore Mann, and José, Quintero. Starting as the Loft Players in a loft (naturally) in Greenwich Village, they evolved into the most acclaimed and solid organization in operation, both OB and on Broadway. Of the original triumvirate, only Mr. Mann remains as producer.

The Circle's 1952 production of *Summer and Smoke* was responsible for OB's total acceptance on its own terms—without condescension—as an original, dynamic theatrical force to be contended with. Director Quintero and leading lady Geraldine Page found qualities in Tennessee Williams' play that had not been realized in its Broadway production. Brooks

Atkinson's review started a stampede of critics led by the late Vernon Rice of the New York *Post,* and afterward they covered OB regularly.

That pattern for success was later repeated with Jason Robards, Jr., in *The Iceman Cometh*. That work was initially unappreciated until the Circle produced it and reviewed the reputation of O'Neill while making a great new one for Robards.

The Circle has bridged the gap between OB and the Main Stem by successfully doing O'Neill and making the queen of Off Broadway, Colleen Dewhurst, a star in both arenas. But the difference between up and downtown is more than geography, and among those who have been completely consumed by attempting the transition were the producers of *The Respectful Prostitute, Hope Is the Thing with Feathers, The Golden Apple,* and *Once upon a Mattress. Hair* is the great exception, but the musical was redone for Broadway and allowed squares to see nude hippies to feel they were with it. Others have recently tried uptown with only mild success. Usually, though, a show that stays downtown has a greater chance for a long run—years, in fact, for *The Three Penny Opera, The Blacks*, and *The Fantasticks*. The loyal followers of OB do not mind inconvenience and discomfort to have their special tastes catered to.

The dedication to present the best of the old and the new to a select few is exemplified by Judith Malina and Julian Beck, the husband and wife producing, directing, and acting team that ran the Living Theatre. The impact of their production of Jack Gelber's *The Connection* was shattering, because it broke the barriers between actors and audience by creating the illusion of an actual happening.

Reality itself gave the company a dramatic exit. The government locked the doors of the theater for nonpayment of taxes. That didn't stop these free thinkers; they herded the audience to the roof of an adjacent building and sneaked them inside for the show. When the law enforcers finally won, the

Lotte Lenya and Scott Merrill in Carmen Capalbo's production of *The Three Penny Opera* (Photograph by Culver Pictures)

The Blacks by Jean Genet, directed by

ene Frankel (Photograph by Richard Marx)

The original cast of *The Fantasticks:* (front row) Jay Hampton, Kenneth Nelson, George Curley, (center row) Hugh Thomas, Rita Gardner, William Larsen, (rear) Jerry Orbach (Zodiac Photographers)

Living Theatre toured Europe. There the group evolved a new style and came back to America several years later to present revolutionary productions that had an improvisational quality and totally involved the audience. So controversial was its effect on the public that dissension arose among the troupe, and upon returning to Europe, the Living Theatre disbanded.

The image that OB presented—quick recognition without too great a financial risk—resulted, by the midsixties, in a rash of vanity productions that quickly let many a rich uncle know there was no real talent in the family. Not only was nepotism rampant, but also neophytism, promulgated by the increasing popularity of fine Absurdist plays, which made many writers think that their own lack of logic could be passed off as art.

After less than a score of years, OB's Golden Era became tarnished. Its public was like an old lover grown tired and restless. Critics expressed disappointment that, except for Albee, no writer of any real stature had emerged, ignoring the fact that neither had any other playwright come full-blown to the Main Stem during that time and that the reputations of Broadway's Williams and Miller were kept alive by OB revivals and not by their current works. And even Jerry Herman, the composer of Broadway's biggest musical hit, *Hello, Dolly!* had started in a little OB revue.

As OB approached sixty-five, it looked as though paralysis was setting in. Producers became immobilized by the growing OB costs and by anxiety to anticipate, rather than initiate, public preferences.

As for the audience, those aging intellectuals who once supported OB were now living in the suburbs, and their youthful replacements felt that this once vigorous theater had a vintage flavor, especially since, to them, OB was expensive and Establishment.

Many of the younger set expressed their break with tradition by creating and attending liberated motion pictures and wild, improvisatory plays Off Off Broadway. The new hybrid of theater was springing up all over Greenwich Village in every kind of place imaginable; for a voluntary contribution or for the price of a cup of coffee, one could see uninhibited plays by unwanted writers with untrained actors in unpretentious productions. All done for next to nothing, as in the days of O'Neill, in an often faltering attempt to find new forms of theatrical expression that would speak the language of the day.

With all those seemingly insurmountable problems, it would appear that the tragic end of OB was inevitable. But once again OB showed that it thrives on adversity. At the turn of the decade, the very factors that almost led to its demise resulted in OB's renaissance.

If OB was being plagued by higher overhead, Broadway was in greater trouble. Panic was rampant uptown when only twelve productions were announced for the first half of the '69 to '70 season. Where had everyone gone? Well, with musicals budgeted at more than $500,000 and straight plays at over $150,000 (and money was no guarantee of success), no wonder producers like Edgar Lansbury, Kermit Bloomgarden, and Herman Shumlin started to look elsewhere. OB offered them the chance to do more venturesome shows at a quarter of the cost and still get equally handsome returns. *Scuba Duba, Boys in the Band,* and *Your Own Thing* showed that big money could be made on a hit not only from the OB run, but also from tours of major theaters throughout the country and from half-million-dollar movie sales as well—all the pluses of a Broadway hit minus the huge risk.

As success breeds success, an excitement prevailed that attracted the middle-class, middle-age audience that was becoming more and more dissatisfied with the sparse fare uptown. These affluent people did not mind paying higher prices to have their egos massaged. To see the nude show *Oh! Calcutta!* and lay out twenty-five dollars for a seat in the first two rows and even more when paying scalpers or on New Year's Eve became a game of oneupmanship. Sex, the more exotic and explicit the better, became a major OB attraction. The climax came when the law prosecuted Lennox Raphael's *Che!* the wildcat show that moved into the OB area and charged ten dollars for the privilege of seeing how far you can go with sex and social significance.

While the bizarre breakthroughs increased OB's popularity, an influx of important productions raised its cultural sights. Joseph Papp's institutional Public Theatre—the original producers of the musical that had the greatest impact of any show in recent time, *Hair*—came up with Charles Gordone's *No Place to Be Somebody*. This play won the 1970 Pulitzer Prize—coincidentally, the second for an OB play on a black theme. The Negro Ensemble Company gave black talent further opportunities with productions of plays on themes of black struggle like *Ceremonies in Dark Old Men* and *The Dream on Monkey Mountain*. Lincoln Center, still trying to find a place for itself in the theatrical world, tried more and more revivals and off-beat shows with an almost OB image. And La Mama E.T.C., the Open Theatre, the now defunct Caffè Cino, and others of Off Off Broadway flowed into OB to capitalize on their productions of *The Dirtiest Show in Town*, *Dames at Sea*, *America Hurrah!*, *The Concept*, and *Futz*, which was directed by Tom O'Horgan who made his mark with *Hair*.

The triumph of the rejuvenated OB was complete in 1970 when downtown houses were almost entirely booked and theaters uptown were going begging. This was also partially due to scarcity of big Broadway investors—the market having fallen—and of movie and record preproduction deals that were once so common. The day had come when even the Shuberts were offering concessions to producers of OB shows to lure them to Broadway houses.

A new air of glamour permeated the OB environs. The

Pulitzer Prize winner was also an OB drama, Paul Zindel's *The Effect of Gamma Rays on Man-in-the-Moon Marigolds.* This play had won the New York Drama Critics Award in 1970. Again, in 1971 this prize went to an OB play, *The House of Blue Leaves*, by John Guare. Recently, in the dramatic department, the typical Broadway offering was the usual Neil Simon comedy, *The Last of the Red Hot Lovers* (which had to go OB for its director and stars, Robert Moore of *Boys in the Band* and Jimmy Coco, Linda Lavin,

Tom Eyen's *The Dirtiest Show in Town* (Photograph © Max Waldman, 1971)

and Marcia Rodd), *Child's Play* (starring OB's Fritz Weaver and directed by Joseph Hardy who made a name for himself with OB's smash, *You're a Good Man, Charlie Brown*), and imports like *Borstal Boy* (which everyone agreed would have thrived better downtown). Young people went OB to see rock musicals, which were literally booming. Their Off Off Broadway was not proving the insurgent force they expected; it had gone respectable and was accepted, in the same way that beards and long hair were. Moreover, its no-text plays, which subjugated word to movement, fostered playwrights who so far have had only a modicum of achievement, the best showing up on OB, anyway. And with stars like Anthony Perkins and Zoe Caldwell appearing, as well as flesh shows, OB was becoming a real tourist attraction.

As a compromise between the downtown David and the uptown Goliath, a new form of theater has been introduced: Middle Theater. These five-hundred-seat houses offer seats at lower prices than Broadway productions and yet give royalty and union concessions that allow producers to make a profit on a gross of $25,000 weekly. This could release 199-seat houses to Off Off Broadway so that it can come out of the laboratory and be more communicative to more people.

How vital OB is to New York theater was dramatically realized at the end of 1970 when the Actor's Equity OB strike for better wages and working conditions closed the downtown theaters for several weeks and there was no new excitement on stages anywhere to compensate. Though, admittedly, there are shortcomings—the commercialism of plays and musicals that would go uptown, the lack of responsibility toward producing the latest works of playwrights like Ionesco and Genêt, the want of daring in not putting on innovative plays except for those being done by such institutions as the

Public Theater and the Chelsea Theater at the Brooklyn Academy of Music—compared to what exists anywhere else, OB is "the best of all possible worlds."

With Broadway reaching out and Off Off Broadway moving up, OB has arrived at the enviable position of being the truly alternate theater. This alteration in status will never be status quo because the premise of OB has always been to welcome change—as has been shown in its five major phases: the introduction through social drama; the art theater image of O'Neill's day; the plays of protest during the Depression; the postwar explosion downtown that gave an important outlet for classical and contemporary plays; and now, side-by-side with Broadway, worthy dramas and musicals that pay off both artistically and financially.

Contributing to OB's achievements have been many notable talents. Among those not mentioned before are such illustrious contemporaries as Kim Stanley, Tammy Grimes, Barbara Harris, Dody Goodman, Carol Burnett, Barbra Streisand, Ruby Dee, Nancy Wickwire, Estelle Parsons, Jane White, Sada Thompson, Inga Swenson, George C. Scott, James Earl Jones, Hal Holbrook, Dustin Hoffman, Ben Gazzara, Robert Hooks, Anthony Franciosa, George Segal, Ron Liebman, Ossie Davis, Mike Nichols, Elaine May, Alan Arkin, William Ball, Jack Garfein, Stuart Vaughan, Gene Saks, Michael Cacoyanis, Gerald Freedman, Gene Frankel, Bruce Jay Friedman, Mary Rodgers, Fred Ebb, Tom Jones, and Harvey Schmidt. For every one of those famous names, thousands of others are unknown and have been absorbed into the mainstream of theater—while thousands of others who never made it have been given their chances to try.

The story of how the eminence of OB was attained is personally told here by outstanding artists in every aspect of theater. The aim is to give inspiration and insight to all theater people with the ambition to attempt, and all theatergoers with the desire to enjoy, the Off-Broadway Experience.

Theodore Mann (Zodiac Photographers)

II

The
Cornerstone:
**THEODORE
MANN**
**and Circle in
the Square**
Better and
Tougher

IN THE summer of 1950, a small group of actors who had been working under the name of the Loft Players in a Greenwich Village loft took over the Maverick Theatre in Woodstock. I happened to be passing through, chasing some girls, and the troupe asked me to be company manager. I had never done that kind of work before, but it appealed to me. We were so successful—the first summer-stock theater that did not go bankrupt at that location in twenty-five years— that we decided to stay together and try to find a theater in New York.

The theaters available in the Village seemed terribly tiny and uninteresting to us. We finally found a Sheridan Square nightclub that was closed, but the real-estate agent wanted a thousand dollars a month rent and a long-term lease. We just couldn't afford it. When I told my father about it, he promised us the first month's rent and offered to negotiate with the agent for us. We signed the lease and began to hire more actors for repertory.

The original Circle in the Square was a couple of adjoining brownstones. There were three floors above the theater. Since we paid everybody only fifteen dollars a week, we used the rooms upstairs as living quarters and assigned each person living there a specific domestic task so we could eat and keep the place clean. Even though we didn't know which plays we were going to do, we worked on raising money and finding sponsors. We got six thousand dollars together and decided to produce *Dark of the Moon*.

Before we had gone into production, we learned we needed a theater license to operate but couldn't get one due to a zoning restriction. So we left the tables in place and applied for a nightclub permit. Until it came through, we couldn't charge admission for our performances, so we made a little speech at the end of each show and passed the basket. This was charming but financially hazardous. Within a few months our money began to dwindle, and a lawyer helped us convince the police that we were not criminals but young kids trying to start a theater. The police relented, issued a nightclub permit, and we began to charge admission and get some favorable notices. But the next few productions did poorly, and we couldn't even pay the small salaries.

By the following summer, many of our company had left. The deprivations were great and the prospects bleak. Those of us who remained toured the Catskills' Borscht Belt in a station wagon I'd bought. We did Christopher Fry's *A Phoenix Too Frequent*. At one of the more highbrow places, we played to four hundred people. The show ran forty-five minutes, and it was a race between our finishing it and the audience getting to the exit. At the end, there were three people left in the theater, applauding like mad. They were the kitchen help. The next day I tried to get our check from the man who ran the hotel. He refused to pay on the grounds that we were terrible. Only by threatening to camp there did we get him to come through with the money.

That fall we returned to our Greenwich Village home and managed to struggle along until we broke through with the show that revolutionized Off Broadway, *Summer and Smoke*— a previous Broadway flop reconceived by our director, José Quintero. Geraldine Page, who became famous as a result of this production, had been jobbed in only once previously to do a small part for us. With this success, two years after we'd started, we abandoned the concept of a repertory company. Until then, we had been restricted to plays which utilized the actors we had available. This limitation is one of the drawbacks of a repertory system in the United States; in Europe, subsidy allows repertory groups to keep a large pool of actors available, but not exclusively, for their productions. It's difficult to determine in advance what ten or fifteen actors would be ideal in any plays you decide to do.

Although we were all still young, we were learning to assess talent properly and to realize our own potential. *Summer*

Geraldine Page in *Summer and Smoke;* Lee Richards and Kathleen Murray to her right (By permission of Circle in the Square)

and Smoke enabled us to pay off our bills, repair the theater, install air-conditioning, and save some money for future productions. It also gave us the chance to fill our ambition to expand. We opened a theater in Philadelphia, which unfortunately did not do well and closed after two plays.

We never had any predetermined concept of what our contribution to the theater was to be. That evolved by doing.

The selection of plays over the last twenty years has been based on the literacy of the material. That has always been our paramount interest. Through the years we have refined our choices, and looking back at the more than fifty plays we have done, our literary level, I believe, has been quite high and meaningful to the public. If any pattern emerges from what we have done, its emphasis is equally divided between presenting important new plays and reexamining the masters.

Our next major success was in 1954—*The Girl on the Via Flaminia*. Everything was going well when the fire department suddenly closed us down. We moved the show to Broadway, but it didn't go over there and closed after a few weeks. We no longer had a home, and only a few of us, including José Quintero and myself, were left from the original company. I took a job working on Franklin Delano Roosevelt, Jr.'s gubernatorial campaign, determined that somehow I would find somebody who could help get the theater reopened. Afterward, Frank's office came through by clearing up our conflict with the fire department. We were home again in 1955, but we weren't drawing at the box office.

By May of 1956, we knew we were going under and decided we might as well sink in glory by choosing the biggest and toughest play we could find: *The Iceman Cometh*—five and a half hours long, with twenty-five actors. We had often tried to get the rights to an O'Neill play with no success. This season I again submitted our annual request to the agent and was anticipating her usual refusal when I heard her say, "Well, which O'Neill play would you like to do?" Unprepared for her response and not sure what she had in mind, I meekly told her, "We'd be happy to do whatever you'd be most likely to let us do"—perhaps one of the lesser known works. She laughed and rephrased it: "If you could choose any O'Neill play you wanted, which would it be?" "*The Iceman*," I replied, and she immediately gave us the rights.

Our first problem was to get an actor to play Hickey. We

hired Howard da Silva, but he didn't really want to do it. Late one night as we wrestled with the casting, Jason Robards, determined to do the part, came in and insisted we couldn't turn him down. José loved his reading. That production cost ten thousand dollars, pretty high for those days, and we didn't have money enough to put it on. We were finally so destitute that I called Roger Stevens, who said he was leaving town but agreed to leave a check for two thousand dollars with his secretary, which pulled us through.

As a result of what José did with *The Iceman*, we got the chance to do *Long Day's Journey into Night* on Broadway. These two successes back-to-back gave us a financial breakthrough and gave the American public an opportunity to re-evaluate O'Neill. We discovered it wasn't difficult to raise the money for Broadway. The main difference, it seemed, between working uptown and downtown was that on Broadway there is departmentalization. But our situation was a little different since we used many of the people who worked with us in the Village, including Leigh Connell, who joined José and myself as producer, David Hays, our scenic designer, and Tharon Musser, our lighting designer.

A couple of years later, when we were forced to get out of the old theater and move into our new one on Bleecker Street, I had the good feeling we were starting all over again. José directed *The Balcony* and three one-acters written especially for us by Thornton Wilder, *Plays for Bleecker Street*. With our new facilities we also founded a theater training school.

About this time, José and I split. As a director I guess he wanted the more expansive satisfaction that he could derive from working on many shows without the confines of one production company. My interests still lay solely with the Circle in the Square.

By the end of 1963, I was running the theater and choosing the plays myself, and finally I turned to directing, too. As I became more involved artistically, Paul Libin joined me and gradually assumed more and more of the producing responsibilities, until now I am directing exclusively.

At last, after years of success at our own home and occasionally at the Martinique Theatre, doing everything from *The Trojan Women* to *Eh!*, which introduced Dustin Hoffman, we at least have a permanent expansion program going. We now present a season of plays each year at the Ford Theater in Washington, D.C., and have a new theater on Broadway which is a larger version of the Circle with 650 seats. The new theater is first class, but costs have been scaled down so that we will be able to sustain ourselves in a modest way.

More is made of rising Off-Broadway production expenses than is warranted, because we must remember that all costs of living have gone up as well. During *Summer and Smoke* we paid the actors twenty-five dollars weekly. Now Off-Broadway salaries start at more than four times that, and with the Equity sliding scale the actor can earn the Broadway minimum if the show is a hit. Advertising rates are higher, and you have to take more space to be noticed today. Rents have increased, but not greatly considering the demand for space. More money is spent on costumes and scenery, and there are professional crews to do physical work—all of which makes for greater quality theater. Shows may be expensive to put on, but that isn't stopping productions from happening.

Dark of the Moon cost us four thousand dollars. Today we bring in a show for thirty thousand dollars, and if we were one-shot producers, it would cost us fifty thousand dollars. Being around for a long time helps, and having a continuity of production and staff gives us an advantage in cutting corners. After twenty years, I think we're better and tougher.

III

The Actor:
JASON ROBARDS
Trust Yourself

I USED to have to write letters to myself saying, "Trust yourself!" I'd sign my own name, and send it special delivery to the theater, so that it was waiting for me on my dressing table on opening night. I did this for *The Iceman Cometh*, too, the play that set me up as an actor when it opened Off Broadway. It was particularly significant for me then, because the two preview audiences didn't react the way we hoped they would. When I read my note to myself, I turned to another actor and said, "You see, we've got nothing to worry about."

Once I decided to become an actor, I always trusted myself. But I had never thought about acting until the last year I was in the Navy. I was brought up mostly removed from the field, even though my father was in pictures. Out on the Coast while I was going to school I was more concerned with the beach and playing ball. I was too young to remember my father's stage work. By the time I was aware of what he was doing, he wasn't doing well, so we didn't talk much about that.

Then in '39 I went into the Navy. It was before the war, and I wanted to go to sea and travel. When the war was over, and I had been in the Navy for seven years, I didn't know what to do. For a while I considered staying in for twenty years and retiring when I was thirty-seven. But what would I do if I got out? I'd only a high-school education, and I didn't want to go back and bum around L.A. I was well equipped to ride a surfboard the rest of my life; however, I didn't want to be the first of the Venice beatniks.

By accident, I picked up a play in the ship's library aboard the cruiser on which I was stationed. I thought it was a novel, but I found out that *Strange Interlude* by Eugene O'Neill was a dramatic work. I became excited by the style of people speaking their thoughts, and it triggered something that must have been lying dormant within myself that I didn't even know was there. Something that I had probably shut off all through my childhood. Something that I had probably heard all my life from my Dad.

Jason Robards

I wrote him a letter and said, "I want to be an actor. What could I do about it, when I got out of the Navy?"

He replied that I should study because I didn't know the first thing about the theater or its history. He recommended that I go to the school that he had gone to in New York and not take up acting in California. He felt that trying to go in and get a stock contract from one of the studios would not help me to learn anything about the business.

He wrote a letter to the American Academy of Dramatic Art, and the same people who were there when he went were still there, but they were now in their seventies. For my audition for them I learned the speech from *The Last Mile* about the prisoner going to his death. I was so nervous that I said all the lines in a hurry, but they said they'd take me.

I was on the G.I. Bill, and that paid for some of my tuition. I went through the first year of history, speech, and interpretation. and all the time we rehearsed and put on plays in front of audiences recruited from the street. These people tell you quickly if you're any good or not. Not like doing plays at a studio where they just come to pick you apart. A few times out, and I fell right into it.

After about a month, they threw us on a stage in a house that had a very bad dead spot. The instructors would yell at you constantly that they couldn't hear you. During the first four weeks, my whole approach changed. I became aware of what I had and of ways to project ideas and words in volume. It became second nature to me to make something extra take place. Even today, I have that energy and I'm not conscious that I'm belting, but I can always be heard, thanks to the way I was taught by old Charles Gellinger to play to the balcony rail.

The sixty dollars a month I got from the G.I. Bill wasn't quite enough, and at the end of the month my friends and I would go to the Automat and eat for nothing by getting hot water and putting catsup on crackers you find on the table.

Once I got through that first year, I went into stock in
Delaware. Tom Poston, who was half a year ahead of me, ran
the company with his brother. They needed an actor to split
the leading roles with Tom—lead one week, support the next—
for the fifteen shows they put on that summer. When they
called the school, I was the one who was recommended for the
job. For thirty-five dollars a week plus room and board I did
everything, including building the set. It was tough.

When I returned to New York, Tom Poston and the
academy helped me again. (Through the years I found that all
my contacts were people who had started at the academy.)
Tom was working for one of the teachers and her husband
who began the Children's World Theatre at the Barbizon Plaza.
It had a lot of money behind it, and turned out to be a very
successful venture. Tom was playing the giant in *Jack and the
Beanstalk*, and there were also a lot of other kids from the
academy in the cast. On his recommendation I was hired to
stage-manage and play the hind end of the cow. This was how
I made my professional stage debut in New York. They didn't
trust me to do the front part of the cow because it required
working the mouth and shaking the head. So I was stuck with
being bent over, cooped up, and I found it extremely difficult
to breathe.

They began to give me other parts to play in their repertory.
We toured Bridgeport, Philadelphia, as well as outlying parts of
New York. Our audiences had built so much that the Skouras
theaters booked us into some of their movie houses before the
Saturday matinees. We actually were reviewed by everybody
and especially by Brooks Atkinson. The critics would take a
child with them, and they would write their reviews from what
the youngster said, adding very little of their own interpretation. They were consistently raves, and I believe the group
deserved them. It was a unique operation that didn't present
the pap that is being presented for children today. We had
good actors and good plays. Typical was *Many Moons* by

James Thurber which was fascinating even for adults. Although we were a children's theater, we weren't kidding around.

The money was so little that I had to get a job instructing at the Theatre School of Dramatic Arts. Again, it was someone from the academy who got me this job, teaching a radio course about which I knew practically nothing. I needed both these jobs just to make a living. I had been married a couple of years and we had a baby. My wife, whom I'd met while we were acting together in summer stock, was also working. She was in window display for Alexander's department store in the Bronx. We were living in the Village and were able to get along, but it was rough. Yet we felt these things would work out.

Then one day I came to work at the school, and there was a lock at the door. Without any warning, the city marshal had closed it. It seemed, the head of the school had absconded with all the funds from the G.I. Bill, and left us with all the money he owed. That was the end of that job.

To keep myself and my family going, I had to go to work for Brown's Steno Service. They'd send me around to various offices as a typist and stenographer. One of the jobs was for an advertising agency which was in the theatrical field. In fact, they were involved in the production of *Stalag 17.* Because of this, I felt more at home with them and stayed there until I went into summer stock. Anytime a job in the theater turned up, I'd quit anything and go anywhere to act.

I did the Grist Mill Playhouse a couple of times, also the Playhouse-in-the-Park, which used to bring in packages from New York, like they do today with big stars, but in those days it was with unknowns like myself.

That kind of struggling went on for the next nine years. One of my best sources of income was my radio work. Through a marvelous lady, Elaine Carrington, who was called queen of the soap operas, I got into three shows: *Pepper Young's Family,*

When a Girl Marries, and the short-lived *Marriage for Two.*
From these came jobs in other soap operas and a running part
as the villain for a year on *Perry Mason.*

I also announced for a while on WINS, doing commercials
on a free-lance basis for Tamarack Lodge and Ben Tucker's
Hudson Bay Fur Company in downtown Brooklyn. I used to
yell out the one that went, "Did you say 557? No, I said 557
South DeKalb Avenue in downtown Brooklyn!" Those were
hard-sell, screaming commercials. They were terrible, and the
producer kept saying, "Nice and loud and strong! Think of
yourself as Hitler!" I started flubbing the minute I did.

I auditioned for NBC for a great guy who was running the
announcing staff, Pat Kelly. I wanted to get into the local New
York station as an announcer, but I just didn't quite make it.
Some time later Pat called and said, "Hey, listen, I got a job
for you on a new station in New Jersey, WPAT." Though he
didn't feel I was ready for New York yet, he thought I could
handle that assignment. My wife and I had to come to a big
decision because the job paid fifteen grand a year, and we had
two kids by then. We realized I'd have to throw over everything to move out there, and it would be the end of the road
as far as acting was concerned. I turned down Pat's offer when
my wife said, "Oh, we might as well keep going; we've gone
this far." So we kept going.

Since the radio and stock work were not steady, I had to
return to being a secretary once in a while, as well as other odd
jobs. One afternoon I was sitting in Central Park during my
lunch hour, and a guy I went to the academy with, and hadn't
seen for a couple of years, came by.

He said, "Listen, I know of a job. It's with a health parlor
on 52nd Street and Eighth Avenue. This woman who runs it
is some kind of health nut, and she needs someone to help
her stretch people to make them taller."

I got the job putting people on a rack like an exercise
table with a sling that went over their feet, and with

crutches on the other end which went under their arms. I'd turn a wheel which would pull their vertebrae apart little by little until they couldn't take it anymore; then I'd put the sling on the head and give it a small turn. They'd hold that position for a while, then I'd measure them on the height machine. They'd gain about two inches which was what they needed to pass their physicals for the police and fire departments. They'd have to tear out of the place and jump into a cab to get to the examinations before they'd shrink back to their normal size.

Each morning before I could work, the woman who ran the place would sit me down and tell my fortune by the cards to see what the day was going to bring. One day she said, "I'm going to Florida, and I want you to run the place for two weeks until I come back."

After a couple of days, when I came to work, I found a lock on the door. Once again, it was the city marshal closing up the phony business in which I was involved.

A lot of times I came close to losing my faith. I was even forced to seek empty bottles in trash cans, so that I could return them to the supermarket for nickels. This way I was able to get together as much as a dollar and a half on some weekends. And, with this, we could buy a lot of meat at the wholesale meat market over which we lived. The stew we made from it would last us for a week. That's the way we got along, raising a family while trying to stay in the theater.

Television was just starting then, and that's how I began to improve my earnings. I got leads on jobs from people I knew. I started with five lines or better, then I moved up to doing leads on some of the top nighttime shows. I played everything: cowboys, villains, doctors, eighty-five-year-old men, newspaper reporters, policemen—you name it, I did it. Those were the great days—television was live and everyone was all wrapped up in doing the most creative jobs possible.

We had fine crews pulling together to win, even though there was always panic because it was live and there was no turning back as there is in film and tape. It was like stock; the only thing lacking was an audience. It required a different kind of acting. I loved it.

All the while I was trying to do other things to get on the stage. Once a group of guys and girls from the academy got together to put on some plays at the 23rd Street YMCA theater which we rented for fifteen dollars a night. That's where I made my Off-Broadway debut in Shaw's *Buoyant Billions* with Colleen Dewhurst, Paul Shyre, Henry Beckman, Jim Vickery, Harding Lemay, and his wife Priscilla. We put up a slipshod set, and we were terrible, I'm sure. The only critic who showed up was Robert Garland of the *Journal-American*. We'd put him to sleep, and he'd wake up and laugh in the wrong places, but at least we had a critic who gave us a review. After a while Vernon Rice and Brooks Atkinson came down to see us and liked what they saw. I feel that both of them are responsible for starting me Off Broadway—especially Brooks.

Then came my first break. Once again Tom Poston was involved. Both he and Don Murray, who was our juvenile in the Delaware stock company and a close friend of mine, got into José Ferrer's production of *The Insect Comedy*. Through that connection they heard that José was casting a play called *The Chase* by Horton Foote. Along with a thousand other people, I went to his office. Thanks to my friends' recommendation, José singled me out and asked me in. I read a few lines for him and Horton, and they gave me the dual job of understudying the lead and being the stage manager.

The show didn't last long, and when it closed, they gave me the same double assignment for another one of their productions, *Stalag 17*. I was with the New York company when they toured the country for the next two years, taking over the lead when it was done at the Playhouse-in-the-Park.

I'd taken my wife and kids with me, and it was difficult to get along on $120 a week with all the expense of hotel living, but we managed and even saved a little money. After being on the road, I came back to New York and was one of the twenty-two guys in the show who were buried because nobody knew what happened to any of us. In the meantime, I'd lost contact with the radio and television people I knew, but I started making the rounds once more, and my agent, Archer King, began placing me in TV again.

There was never a secure income; it was up one week and down the next. The pay scale was very low in those days, though I'd get fifty bucks over that which was nothing. I'd never know in a three-month period whether I'd do one show or five shows. I'd do readings for TV constantly while still trying to get into Broadway shows, which was a closed door. I did two nights' extra work in the movie *The Shrike* that José Ferrer threw to Tom Poston and me so that we could earn a few extra bucks. I continued to do stock whenever I could, just to keep acting. Although the TV pay was higher, I'd give it up for a week of stage jobbing just to do a play.

For three years I went along like that. We'd owe money, we'd pay our debts, and we were always trying to break even. My wife and I agreed that you had to be happy in what you do; if you love your work, it makes for a better life even if you don't have everything. It's no good to force yourself into doing something that could drive you crazy. I turned down another job to run a radio station at a good salary. To help, my wife worked off and on, and we got by.

Aside from attending Uta Hagen's acting class once a week on lower Fifth Avenue, I didn't have anything regular to do. One afternoon I went into Jack Barry's bar on Greenwich Avenue just to have a beer, and the barmaid, with whom I'd been in stock, said, "I'm working for José Quintero in the evenings. We've just finished the run of *Dark of the Moon*. He's getting *The Grass Harp* ready. Why don't you go over and see him?"

I replied, "I don't know him or anything about him."

She said, "Well, go on over to the Circle in the Square, and tell José that I sent you."

Without even finishing my beer, I walked over and got an interview with him. He was looking for someone to replace a guy about fifty.

He had me read and said, "I don't know. I think you're too young. We have too many young people playing old parts. I'm looking for someone a little older, but give me your phone number, and I'll let you do it if I can't find him." He found him.

Six months later the phone rang, and it was José saying, "I've got a play, and I want you for the fellow." He put it just like that.

I got the part in *American Gothic* without reading for it. He remembered that time I'd seen him for only ten minutes. I couldn't believe it when he called me, but that was José's way. By then I was really swinging in TV and radio, getting cast at least once every two weeks. So when he asked, "Look, we don't pay any money. What do you need to get by for food and rent?" I told him, "About sixty-five dollars a week." He said, "I'll take it up with the board of directors." He had nothing to do with the business policy. He was only responsible for artistic choices and the directing. Ted Mann and Leigh Connell were the ones who handled the money. Until this production, they were paying their actors fifteen dollars a week, five of which went for food and for rent for the building in which they all lived. They were forced to move out when the building commissioner declared the place unsafe to live in. They were allowed, however, to keep their offices and theater there.

American Gothic was a strange play and, as it turned out, one of the best jobs of directing that José ever did. It was adapted by Victor Wolfson from his own novel, *The Lonely Steeple*. Victor did a pretty good job, but he didn't quite solve it for the stage. Not that we were in trouble during rehearsal because, I feel, many plays I've done are improved by the play-wrights through their learning what goes and what doesn't. The actors aren't trying to change it; you just see what works. Victor was unwilling to do a lot of things, and so José dismissed him from rehearsal. We went on to do the play as it was written. I think it could have been improved if the writer had been there. The play was not a success. We ran seventy-seven performances. But I enjoyed working at the old Circle in the Square. The setup that José had down there was exciting.

After *Gothic* closed, and they went into *The Girl on the Via Flaminia*, a tremendous hit for them, I got hot again on television. In fact, I was doing an important show for Philco when my big break in *The Iceman Cometh* came up.

I was on my way to rehearsal for Philco and stopped to buy the paper at the stand on the corner of Hudson and Jane streets because my friend, James Green, who had been in *American Gothic* with me, was the vendor. I did this every day to talk to Jim, and that particular morning he said, "Listen, I just heard something. José is doing *The Iceman Cometh;* why don't you try to get in?"

I shouted, "Jesus, let's go, man!" I dashed over to the Circle, not caring that I would be late for the TV show.

When I got to the theater, José confirmed the fact that they were going to do the show, but he said, "I'm seeing a lot of guys." I wasn't a personal friend of his.

"I must be in that play," I insisted. "I've got to play Hickey." Why I felt this way was that I had seen the original production twice, bad as it was. I was at the academy the first time, and we were allowed in the Theatre Guild to make up one of the preview audiences. Then when E. G. Marshall took over for James Barton, I went to see it on my own. O'Neill, unsure of Barton, had wanted E. G. to move into the part before the opening. Though it wasn't successful, the play hit me very deeply, especially that part, yet I never consciously thought of it for myself until I heard about this revival.

Scene from Circle in the Square's production of *The Iceman Cometh* with Farrell Pelly, Jason Robards, Albert Lewis, and Phil Pheffer (Photograph by Jerry Dantzic)

When I repeated, "I've got to play Hickey," José answered, "Well, you're too young for that. I'd like you for Will Oban." Willy was the young lawyer who sang songs all the time and was in the worst shape of all. The character was modeled after O'Neill's older brother at the age of thirty-five or so. E.G. had played it before doing Hickey in the first production. I tried to convince him, "No, I really want to play the other part."

He told me, "There are so many people coming, I really have my pick of actors for Hickey. I'll have to ask you to read, though I don't want to do it." He was apologetic because he thought it was an insult, I guess, but I agreed.

For a couple of days I studied a section which I thought showed most of the elements of Hickey in one speech. When I did it for José, he was stunned a bit, and asked me, "Read right at the beginning—some of that happy stuff." After doing that, he told me, "I'll let you know by six o'clock tonight."

Knowing José, I figured it was his polite way of passing me over. So, I went right next door to Louie's and got a couple of drinks, and in about a half hour, I returned saying, "You better let me know by six o'clock tonight, dammit!" With the false courage of the drinks, I was able to order him.

By God, at five minutes to six, he called up to tell me I had the part of Hickey. That was the start of it.

I knew Hickey's monologue when I went into rehearsal. I figured I should learn it before because it is the greatest background of the character. Usually, you have to pick through a play to find a line here and a line there, and use your imagination to create what a character is, where he came from, and all the things that influenced his life. In that speech, O'Neill wrote the whole thing right out. I always prefer to study the long monologues, which I often seem to get, alone. I think you have to learn those mechanically before you can start working them on stage. I can't learn dialogue, however, until I meet the people with whom I'm going to do it. There's no point in learning something with one idea in mind, and suddenly meeting someone who's playing his role completely differently. The minute you get out of your room and your own mind, all your responses change. I've seen many actors who learn plays before rehearsal, but I won't do it until I get there. I may study a play and read it over and over, until I have absolute familiarity with it; but I won't commit it before it is connected with the behavior of other actors and the moves that are made, so that my interpretation comes out of something specifically. At that point, there is no trouble in learning the part.

That's always been my way. Even when I had to learn the lengthy lead in *After the Fall*, I had no trouble at all memorizing it in ten days. Once we broke it down, had our discussions, staged it carefully, and got it on its feet, the whole thing went right into my head. The same thing happened with *The Iceman Cometh*, except for that speech where he never shuts up—I think it's pretty rare when you get that sort of form. When he appears in the fourth act and starts, even though he is interrupted at one stretch by Jimmy Tomorrow and Harry Hope, Hickey is not listening to anyone. He still keeps going as if it was one speech all the way through.

Iceman is the best play I've ever been in. The satisfaction of doing it was its own reward. I've never gone into the theater or done anything except for the happiness it gave me. I never thought of being a star, of making a success or getting lots of money. Just enough to get by, to eat, to live were my only concerns. That is why I enjoyed stock so much. We ate, had a little fun, and worked on plays. That was everything. Actually, Hickey is not the biggest part. Larry and Rocky are the leads, and never leave the stage. Hickey only comes in five minutes at the end of the first act, twenty minutes in the second, thirty in the third, but in the fourth he goes most of the time. It's a great setup.

I had to miss the first week of rehearsal, because of my job on the Philco show. We had only three weeks to get *The Iceman* on. During this time, they were putting new seats in the theater, which were expensive. Everybody told us the show was going to be a flop. They said, "You can't do that. O'Neill is dead. My God, nobody's been doing that crap since the last bomb, and here you're trying to revive it. You must be out of your head; and to top it off you're borrowing money to put in three thousand dollars worth of seats. You might have to close the theater, and it would be the end of the Circle." That was what José was getting on one side; but he, Ted Mann, and Leigh Connell pushed right through.

The play runs about five and a half hours, but to pull a couple of things together, José did very slight cuts—so well that the author's representative didn't realize it. Nothing was omitted from the first act, because it was a buildup, and José wanted to make a great bubble out of it by playing for comic values so that the tragedy would even be greater when the buoyancy burst. At first, everyone was afraid of this, but then they realized that, when the play was originally done on Broadway, it had begun like the end of the play and had had nowhere to go.

We got to the point in rehearsal where we couldn't make the play move beyond the third act. We felt we'd shot the whole bolt, and it couldn't go further without seeming to be the same thing repeated. José and I talked about it, and he said, "Something's wrong and I can't seem to figure it out. We have to reshape our thinking."

We tried for a different attitude and way of staging, and it worked. Our problem had been how to get into the symbolic death of the characters at the end of the third act, so that the fourth act would be meaningful. All the people start to fade, and we had to walk a tightrope as this happened, especially since Hickey had to catch that feeling from Harry and do something about it in his big speech near the end of the play. It all came together when we realized that Hugo, the guy who kept waking and yelling, "Hang him by the lamppost," had the clue that solved the action. In reexamining the moment that he showed his true colors and screamed in the darkness, we found the key to our answer: the audience had to know that Harry became aware of the disintegration all around him, so that they'd become provoked about what the result would be.

The fourth act was staged only two days before the opening, which took place in the afternoon. I was getting ready for my last entrance, putting shadows under my eyes and blue on the beard to make me look more dissipated than I looked in the other acts, since I was supposed to be up three days, when

I heard a tremendous applause and screaming and yelling. "Oh, my God," I thought, "they imagine the play is over."

I ran out of the dressing room, which was down near the coatroom, through the lobby and to the stairs that led to the stage. José was standing there, and I shouted, "What the hell has happened? Do they think it's the end?"

"No, no," he laughed, "it's a damn symphony!"

The audience had gotten up to cheer when the lights had gone on for the fourth act. The ovation lasted about a minute, and the actors told me afterward that they were pretty shook because they hadn't expected anything like that. It almost threw them from sustaining the mood of that final dirge.

When I came on ten minutes later, in a scene where Rocky, played by Peter Falk, was trying to get Larry to be a pimp, my cue was "Don't let that son of a bitch come near. I'll kill him. He won't have to go to the chair." Then I walk over, put my hat down, and he jumps a foot. Just before he made the jump, he whispered, "We got 'em, Jase, don't screw up the mono- logue!" (He always gave me a little tip every night. Sometimes he'd say, "Crap, they're dying out there, already. Put the coal to it. Run it fast.") Then, I knocked the hell out of it!

Acting is strange. You are split in many ways. You have about six things going in your head. You have to be com- pletely in it, yet aware of the situation and the audience. It's all there if you trust yourself, and I got my letter to do just that. I was cool because I never let myself get tied up in a way that restricts what you can do, that cuts your voice, and that gets everything off point. I had said to myself, "We've done all the work we could, and what the hell, if they don't like it—tough!"

After the opening was over at seven o'clock, we went home to wait for the reviews to come out at eleven. We were to come back then for some chow, and to hear Ted Mann stand up and read what the critics had to say, which was his bit that he liked to go through with every show.

I came back to the theater, all cleaned up, about ten, had something to eat and a couple of drinks. Then, I said to a friend, "Oh, this is a lot of bull, waiting for the reviews like a Broadway opening. It's so noisy down here, let's go next door to Louie's and have a beer." We'd only been gone twenty minutes, but when we came back, Ted had already read the reviews, and everyone was excited because we were a big hit.

The success was a combination of many things. Not only was it the quality of our production but also because O'Neill was being revived in New York after ten years, and there were a lot of articles written about it. *A Moon for the Misbegotten* had been tried out of town and had closed before hitting New York.

I was in this production six months, and it was a wonderful experience. The audience response was great. We never lost a customer. (I call members of the audience that because they pay.) They got so hooked in that theater—which used to be a bar and still had an actual one in the lobby, giving an extra dimension to the saloon setting of the play—that they stayed on after the curtain calls. We had no curtain. We did it all by lights, Black! The actors would clear in the dark, and when the house lights would come up, the audience would still be sitting there.

As we played it, we learned more and improved. José came back a lot, which was very helpful and unusual, since most directors rarely do this, having given their all before the opening. José however, wanted to clear up some things. O'Neill is a unique writer. You can play him for a year or two, as I did in *Long Day's Journey,* and still find new areas to solve, which makes him fascinating to act.

I could only do TV on my one night off, Monday, *Studio One* night. I found that doing *Iceman* was all that I could do. I didn't want anything else. It would take me a few hours to get out of it and relax as well as to get prepared for it. It ran from 7:30 till nearly one in the morning; we didn't have matinees, and we never had a dinner break. We played it straight through, which was much better. I'd get myself ready to be at the theater at 6:30 every night. I cared so much about this show, so delighted and involved in it, that when I did a *Studio One* my mind was on *Iceman*.

I left it when we were in rehearsal for the Broadway production of *Long Day's Journey into Night*. A couple of weeks after *Iceman* had opened, Mrs. O'Neill called up José, and in appreciation of his reviving the public's interest in her husband's work, offered him this new play. I went with José to her apartment off Madison Avenue in the sixties. José had been up there before and asked me to go along this time, telling me, "It's a kind of mysterious experience."

The room was very dark, and there were pictures of O'Neill around. His widow was all in black. She was very sweet, gave me a big kiss, and thanked me. We talked about her husband and Hickey. She recalled the opening of the original New York production of *Iceman* and how O'Neill stayed home because he knew it was not going to go well. He had realized from the rehearsals that it wouldn't work.

Speaking with her was like taking a sentimental journey into the past; she was living back then. She told us she was entrusting *Long Day's Journey* to us because of the way we did *Iceman*. I will never forget the forty-five minutes we spent with Mrs. O'Neill.

Originally, I was to play the younger brother, patterned after Eugene himself, in *Long Day's Journey*. Even though he was twenty-four, he was so shot he looked forty. Once again, I had to tell José that I wanted to play a role other than the one he wanted me for, that of Jamie, the older brother. This time he was completely agreeable, and that's the part that began my career on Broadway.

It took me ten years to reach that. I never gave myself any deadline; I didn't know if it would ever happen, and I didn't care, just as long as I could work. I can't go without acting.

The beach or fishing may be okay for some, but my pleasure is acting.

I never doubted myself, even when those preview audiences almost folded us because they were so against *Iceman*. People came to me to put it down, and I wouldn't listen to them. José knew that we were right, and I felt the same way. They talked to me about acting problems. I'm not interested in those things. I've never been much of a student. The only thing I'm concerned with is if the content gets across to the audience, and I've been in the business long enough to know when a play works. It doesn't matter whether they love it or hate it, just so long as they're not indifferent. Making that happen is part of my instrument as an actor, and I don't question it.

If I started to examine what the hell acting is all about, I'd be like some of those unsuccessful actors who run classes. They probe so much that they can't act anymore. I always felt I had to get up on a stage and perform before people; studying didn't matter. I believe in going before the public because you can't really act unless you have an audience. The only advice I have for young people is, no matter how you do it, do it in front of people who pay. It's the paying public who'll tell you if you've got it. This kind of exposure has built my belief in myself.

Getting a serious play on Broadway is very difficult. I've had that battle to fight. I try to do a different kind of play every time to shake up the theater. If I had to do commercial crap, I'd kill myself in three months or else get on a boat and disappear.

Broadway is like military life. They run an act to the minute, using a stopwatch. I remember once knocking ten seconds off an act because the director insisted. At least in motion pictures you can run a few days over the schedule. Broadway is all high finance, a five-hundred-to-one shot that you'll make it. That's why there's so much pressure and no freedom.

I'd have done *We Bombed in New Haven* Off Broadway if it weren't for the author's preference. Then we would have had greater freedom and not have been involved with economics. The audiences would have been there by choice, not corralled, whipped into the slaughterhouse, the way Broadway audiences are. After a while, shows that run on Broadway a long time exhaust their real audience and just get tourists that come in and stay at the West Side Motor Inn and the Americana; often they don't have the vaguest idea of what serious plays are about. Off Broadway you don't have to worry about the size of the house and the tremendous price people pay for seats.

Agents think that appearing there is a step down; they don't like me to do plays anywhere. They push the movie work. I'm always bucking them. I trust myself.

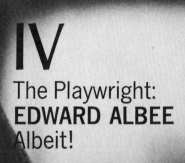

IV
The Playwright:
EDWARD ALBEE
Albeit!

I DECIDED when I was six years old that I was *going to be* a writer. Since this awareness was made one year before the age of reason, as recognized by the Roman Church, I question whether I was *going to be* is as accurate a description of that realization as I *was* a writer. Whichever, it seemed the most natural thing in the world to me. Perhaps I thought it was going to be a lot of fun or perhaps I thought it would be easier than working, but I never thought of myself as anything else other than a writer.

I've held to that for the thirty-three years since then, with the exception of six months when I was eleven and a half and thought I was going to be a composer of serious music. This ambition didn't get anywhere because I couldn't learn how to read music, which made it sort of difficult. It stopped me, though it wouldn't necessarily have stopped other people.

I wrote poetry for twenty years and quit when I was twenty-six. Over that time the poetry got better. It was bound to improve a little, but I didn't think it was good enough to make a career of it. At fifteen, I took time out to write eight hundred pages of one of the worst novels ever written, and at seventeen and a half, I wrote four hundred and some odd pages of another one of the worst novels ever written. I also tried my hand at short stories. I knew that essays weren't for me, because of my typically disorganized, creative mind.

So, at twenty-nine I found myself having attempted two incredibly bad novels, having worked for twenty years on poetry of which I didn't think too much, and having written a few short stories which didn't impress me particularly. Having made up my mind, however, that I was a writer, there really wasn't much left to try except writing plays—which I did more or less by default.

I studied playwriting as little as possible. I think it's criminal to take such courses. I'm not suggesting that they're all fraudulent, though the majority of them are. The only thing someone can teach is either how to write for the instructor or how to

Edward Albee (Photograph by Miss Alix Jeffry)

write like somebody else, neither of which do any good. The only way to learn the art and craft of playwriting is to read hundreds of plays, good and bad, and see hundreds of plays, good and bad. If you make any sense out of that groundwork, add to it a kind of dramatic intuition, plus a certain amount of creative ability, then you have a chance of writing at least one play—not necessarily of getting anywhere as a playwright, though.

Playwriting seemed natural to me, but then again so did poetry and novel writing. The incentive to focus on plays was the certain degree of success I immediately achieved.

My first play was *The Zoo Story*, written in about three weeks as a sort of thirtieth-birthday present to myself.

I had no idea what it felt like to write a play before this, so I can't really say whether I thought I had command of the form. I didn't even know whether I was doing it well or badly. It just seemed perfectly natural, but, as I said, all writing seemed that way to me.

I have absolutely no idea what inspired *The Zoo Story*. I doubt that very many writers can tell what brings about the genesis of any particular work. I look upon this play as many things. I hope that it has more than one possible level of interpretation. I've read about six hundred of them; all the interesting ones seem valid to me. I'm committed to the play itself. I think it speaks fairly clearly, and if it speaks in several tongues, all to the good.

Once *The Zoo Story* was completed, I didn't know quite what to do with it. I showed it to some of my friends. In those days, as well as now, I knew a great many people who were serious composers, a holdover from the time I was going to be one—I do find them to be terribly bright and interesting people, as well. When Aaron Copland, David Diamond, Ned Rorem, and William Flannigan read *The Zoo Story*, they were unanimously encouraging.

William Daniels and George Maharis in Edward Albee's *The Zoo Story*

William Flannigan even sent the play to William Inge who wrote me a nice letter about it. It was Flannigan, also, who sent it to David Diamond, then living in Florence.

David liked it so much he forwarded it to a friend of his, a Swiss-German actor living in Switzerland, named Pincus Brown. He made a tape recording of it, translating it into German as he went along. This he sent to Stefanie Hunzinger, who was head of the Drama Department of the S. Fischer Publishing Company in Frankfurt. The tape impressed her, and she bought the play for German production, doing it in West Berlin on a double bill with Samuel Beckett's *Krapp's Last Tape*.

The world premiere of my first one-act play was in September of 1959, about six months after I wrote it. I'm told that the average amount of time it takes a playwright from the time he writes his first play until the time he gets his first production is usually something like six years. I managed to cut that.

Because of the success of the German production, the play was bought instantly to be staged in New York Off Broadway. Even while it was being rehearsed in Berlin, somebody sent it to the William Morris Agency. At that time, Edward Peron was working in the play-reading department. It was he who brought it to the attention of Richard Barr, who produced it in January of 1960, again on a double bill with *Krapp's Last Tape*.

During the production we ran into a crisis, which, I suppose, is not unusual in the theater. We fired the director after about two weeks, which was the week before opening. His concept of what the play was about and mine were finally seen as too divergent. Dick and I finished the directing, but we did keep the original director's name on the program. He got the credit for the direction which, indeed, was some of his work. The play was so favorably received it ran for about two and a half years. I wasn't surprised at the reaction; I thought it was bound to happen, just as I think if you decide to be a play-wright, your plays will be produced.

Until the initial production of *The Zoo Story*, I worked at various jobs—nothing that was particularly interesting, nothing that would become a career. The only one I enjoyed was delivering telegrams for Western Union, which I did for over two years. It was a pleasant job, even though it didn't pay very well. I liked walking around New York; it took me out into the air, and I appreciated that. Besides, it didn't involve much thinking, so I could concentrate on whatever I wanted to; also, I did meet all sorts of fascinating people, and I was very good at getting tips.

This was the last job I had before becoming a full-time writer for a living. Earning a little money from my writing was nice. I was interviewed occasionally by newspapers and developed a certain amount of moderate celebrity. My life didn't change particularly. I just kept right on writing, which is what I've done up to the present time.

Gian Carlo Menotti, who was producing *Album Leaves*, a series of pieces under fifteen minutes, for the Spoleto festival, approached me to write one of them. At that time I was involved in *The American Dream*, so I took some of the characters out of that play, put them in a slightly different situation, and wrote a shorter work called *Sandbox*. Though it was never done at Spoleto, for one reason or another, it was produced Off Broadway while I was still working on *The American Dream*.

Both *The American Dream* and *The Death of Bessie Smith* were done in Germany before the American productions by the same group that first did *The Zoo Story*. When *The American Dream* came to Off Broadway, it was presented with the opera *Bartleby*. I'd read the libretto which was being written by somebody else who fell ill, so I took over finishing it, but that's a minor matter, since I didn't do much work on it. The dramatic half of the program was well received, but the opera, unfortunately, was not. It was taken off and *The Death of Bessie Smith* was put on in its stead. This double bill ran for a year and a half.

I have a problem of remembering my state of mind from one year to the next. After a certain amount of time, I can't recall the experience of writing any of my plays. That's why I never revise them. I'm not able to put myself in that frame of mind again. I don't recollect my reactions or any anecdotes during rehearsals. I'm too busy watching the play go from the page to the stage to do much of anything except concentrate on making sure that the play being done resembles what I intended when I wrote it down. I've been quite fortunate in that most of my plays do.

At this point, I really should mention one thing for the benefit of people who really do want to be playwrights. That is, they should keep on top of their minds an understanding of their contracts. If they're properly drawn, contracts give the authors a number of very important authorities. The playwright not only chooses who is going to produce his play, but also he has complete control over who the actors are going to be, who the director will be, and what the set is going to look like. And if playwrights will remember to exercise their authority with a certain humility—not to be browbeaten by prima-donna actors, powerhouse directors, or producers who think they're actors, directors, and playwrights—they can emerge from productions with plays that fulfill their aims (for better or worse). I have found that I prefer to have a play of mine staged as I see it. That way I can take the credit myself or bear the blame myself. Too many young playwrights, however, perhaps out of naïveté, greed, or lack of self-confidence, throw off too much of their responsibilities and their powers. That way they end up with something that doesn't belong to them. It's extremely important that they remember what they can do and hold fast to it.

I once made the experiment of changing a script to accommodate the actors and the director, to see if that would produce satisfying results. It was with *Malcolm*, as a matter of fact. This was my second adaptation of a book; the first was *The Ballad of the Sad Café* which followed *Who's Afraid of Virginia Woolf?* The reason I did *Sad Café* and *Malcolm* is that I don't like the way most novels are dramatized, and I was interested in the experience of taking a book from the original writer's hands and translating it to the stage. With *Sad Café* it worked, but doing *Malcolm* may have been a bad idea in the first place. The alterations that were made during productions, however, proved to me that pleasing others does not lead to one's best work. I do think the original script was a good deal better than what finally emerged onstage. But I don't want to beat a dead *Malcolm*.

I'm always writing two or three plays in one fashion or another. I discover that I have been thinking about a play, and then I toss the idea around for maybe six months to two years, letting it develop as it wants to and stew, so to speak. Finally, when the play is completely organized in my mind, a day does come to go to the typewriter and write it down. The actual writing takes a fairly short amount of time, maybe two or three months for one of the long plays, or maybe a couple of weeks for one of the short ones. When I do write, I generally begin in the morning and work for five hours. I don't rewrite very much. I make one typed script, and when I finish the play, I'll retype it, making a few minor changes, and that's usually the script with which I go into rehearsals. Most times the play opens with a version not very far removed from the original typed script. Maybe I'll cut or add a page or two, but I don't make major changes.

I get everything by osmosis. I don't intellectualize what I do receive. Certainly, being in theaters, watching rehearsals, over-seeing productions, and viewing other people's efforts has given me insight that undoubtedly has had some effect on my work after the original script.

When I started writing *Who's Afraid of Virginia Woolf?* I did not know whether it would be a short or a long play, nor did I have any idea where it would be done. After I finished it, I gave it to my producers, Richard Barr and Clinton Wilder, and the director, Alan Schneider. There was some talk about doing it Off Broadway. The hesitancy of doing a Broadway produc-tion was overcome when they realized they could do it very inexpensively; as it was, they did it for half the usual cost of a Broadway production. Still, it was considered a risk until after the opening.

A play as controversial as *Virginia Woolf* gives vent to a lot of strange speculations. Typical was the rumor that the play was originally intended for four men. I think some crazy old lady in New Jersey wrote this idea in a letter that was published in *The New York Times*. Other people picked it up for fun and games, as well as gossip. There is no truth to it. I wrote it for two men and two women. I don't think it would work the other way, but it might be interesting to see such a production, even though it would look sort of peculiar.

I refuse to talk at all about the meanings of my plays, the intentions, what prompted them or even stylistic matters. I find it best for a writer not to examine such things too closely, because he could become terribly self-conscious about his work. The only blanket statement I will make is that the style and the content of my writing codetermine each other, and if it's working properly, it all ends up not specifically naturalism but absolute realism.

In the light of the critical reaction to *Tiny Alice*, that statement may seem contradictory. Several critics, whose minds may not be able to grasp very much, told the audience that they would have a great deal of trouble understanding the play. This was misleading them, it seems to me, because I do find our audience is more intelligent, at least more perceptive, than the majority of our critics. At the previews of this play, before the critics came, the audiences seemed to be comprehending it perfectly well, but the minute the critics told them they wouldn't—they didn't!

With the great deal of money coming in from *Virginia Woolf*, which the government would take unless we spent it intelligently by supporting a project we believed in, my partners, Barr and Wilder, and I, about six years ago, decided to try to be of some assistance to the Off-Broadway theater where the three of us had such a good time for so many years. We set up an organization called the Playwright's Unit.

We took a theater Off Broadway, and we gathered together, out of the thousands of scripts that we'd all read during the past six or seven years, thirty-five young playwrights. Others wishing to apply sent us scripts. To this day we get a thousand or two thousand a year which are terrible, because most plays that everybody writes are absolutely terrible. The fact that we managed to cull thirty-five people out of maybe thirty-five hundred suggests that maybe one in a hundred of the plays we read was any good. Of these thirty-five I don't suspect that more than three or four are ever going to have any lasting serious careers as playwrights. That's one out of a thousand who are trying, but that's not bad. It's about average for any culture at any time.

Those we've chosen are given the theater to work in, and we get actors and directors for them, as well as audiences. Everybody contributes his talents without pay, and these young playwrights can experiment and see their plays staged without the critics. They can do works in progress; they can do complete works. It's a laboratory for them to make intelligent mistakes and brave adventures before they have to face the commercial world of the theater.

If they want critical assistance, we give it to them. They are most receptive to it, I find, when they see their work on stage. You learn most by doing, much more than by having people tell you what you've done.

This plan has worked out quite well. A number of our playwrights like LeRoi Jones, Adrienne Kennedy, Lanford Wilson, Sam Shepard, and Jean-Claude van Itallie have gone on to a certain amount of success and notoriety as well. Our playwrights have no ties to us. If we like a play well enough at the Playwright's Unit, we'll produce it Off Broadway, or conceivably on Broadway, but they're not committed to us in any fashion.

Although it's fun down there, it's expensive to run. The first three years Barr and Wilder and I were putting our own money into it. That started running a little low, and so the Rockefeller Foundation has given us funds for the next three years in matching grants. I must say that we have to find contributions to go with it.

I'm deeply involved in the economics of Off Broadway as both playwright and producer. Nobody is in this form of theater to make any money, because there's not any money to make. If a playwright can earn $150 to $200 a week, that's all to the good. No producer would do a play Off Broadway expecting to make a profit. I believe that one out of every fifty productions does come out ahead. Even the actors don't get paid very much. People work Off Broadway because it's good theater, and it's interesting. Off Off Broadway is even more interesting, more adventurous, and they rely on contributions to get paid.

I have found that I usually see better plays Off Broadway than I see on Broadway, and I have even a better time Off Off Broadway in café theaters and workshops.

Playwrights should learn as much as they can about everything in every branch of the theater; it can be very useful and of great benefit to them. If you can become a producer of your own plays, you have even that much more control of what's going on than you would otherwise.

I'm only ten plays old, so to speak. I don't know if I am fulfilled in this direction, but I'm a working playwright. I have no idea what I'll be doing ten years from now. I'd rather be writing than anything else. I can't think of any other work I'd prefer doing. I enjoy writing, and I'm happier when I'm at it than when I'm not. I have no particular complaints; some plays have run longer than others.

If this has been mostly factual, it's because I'd rather not deal in other matters—it's wise not to.

Alan Schneider (Photograph by George de Vincent)

V

The Director:
ALAN SCHNEIDER
The Human Scale

THE IDEA of working Off Broadway came to me as a salvation and an answer when I was at an absolute dead end on Broadway. Not only was I being bypassed for jobs, but also the plays that I was offered to direct were commercial comedies from people who had associated me with my original successes, *The Remarkable Mr. Pennypacker* and *Anastasia*. They thought family comedies or romantic melodramas were all that I was capable of directing. Gradually, I was acquiring the reputation of being the poor man's Josh Logan.

My career started in the regional theater. After graduating from college, I worked short stints as radio announcer, freelance writer, and public-relations man. Then I got an M.A. in theater and turned to directing at the Catholic University in Washington, D.C., which happened to be more or less my hometown.

I had never intended to come to New York, but somehow I was offered a chance to make my directorial debut there almost, but not quite, Off Broadway. I directed an American adaption of Maxim Gorki's *Lower Depths*, called *A Long Way from Home*, which was set in a Negro flophouse in South Carolina. This was done for the Experimental Theatre of the American National Theatre and Academy back in 1948. Although the Maxine Elliott in which it was presented was in close proximity to Broadway, being on West 39th Street, the production wasn't what would be called a Broadway enterprise. Yet, it wasn't as far Off Broadway as plays being done in Greenwich Village.

Afterward, I returned to working at the university, England, and other places. Fortunately for me, one of our students at Catholic University helped found the Washington Arena Stage, and I was eventually to become its artistic director. Most of my work, for the next few years, was with this theater. I also directed for other regional theaters throughout the country, as well as the Neighborhood Playhouse in New York, wherever I could. The reputation I had built during this time then led to my first directorial assignment on Broadway, *The Remarkable Mr. Pennypacker*.

Samuel Beckett's *Waiting for Godot,* revived Off Broadway in 1971 with Anthony Holland, David Jay, Paul B. Price, and Henderson Forsythe under the direction of Alan Schneider (Photograph by Miss Alix Jeffry)

Five years later, for various typical and untypical reasons, my career was at a full stop. That's when I came to Off Broadway, or rather to Samuel Beckett.

I had directed *Waiting for Godot* in its American premiere at the Coconut Grove Playhouse in Florida. The play and the production were such a flop that audiences walked out, and all the critics panned it. I thought it was great.

Through that play I made an association with Samuel Beckett. For reasons best known to him, because of his nature as a marvelous human being, instead of going with the Broadway producer of *Godot* on his next play, he stuck with me. At my request, Sam allowed me to buy the rights to *Endgame*. This, despite the fact that I had been associated with, though not necessarily the cause of, the "failure" of *Godot*.

There I was with the production rights to something even more difficult than *Godot—Endgame*. Where does one put on such a play? Obviously, I was determined that it not get the negative reception that *Godot* had received when it opened in New York. And since I did not think *Godot* should have been done on Broadway—a belief finally vindicated by the success of my Off-Broadway revival of that masterpiece—I didn't peddle *Endgame* around that area.

This happened to be the period when foreign and avant-garde plays were being done Off Broadway. I realized that *Endgame* was going to have a limited audience, but then Beckett never has had a mass appeal. And I felt that by doing this play for that audience, I would be able to have complete artistic control of every aspect of production, from casting through previews. I was not listed as the producer, because I didn't want to be, but I actually did coproduce *Endgame* with the then owner of the Cherry Lane Theatre. I had chosen this particular house because it seemed to offer better facilities physically and therefore psychologically. Happily, the owner of the theater also appreciated *Endgame* as much as I did.

Endgame was a production of which I was and still am reasonably proud. The reception for Beckett this time was much more respectful. Favorable notices came from almost everyone, especially from Brooks Atkinson.

Of course, some compromises had to be made in doing this show on a limited budget. However, they were much less than those that Broadway forces upon you. Broadway costs make technical experimentation prohibitive; the pressures for success on the Main Stem normally result in tense, chaotic working conditions. You may have better actors uptown, but the ones that you want are not always available when you want them. Off Broadway attracts actors who are more willing to do an offbeat play or part and to work together.

Sure, Orson Welles would have been a marvelous Hamm, but who could get him? And after we got him, would he have done as well and faithfully as Lester Rawlins? I could not have changed our Clove, Alvin Epstein, for the better. Our Nagg and Nell, Nydia Westman and P. J. Kelly, the oldest living member of Actors' Equity, were absolutely beautiful. They could not be improved upon, nor have I ever seen those parts more beautifully played.

Endgame came as close to my original vision and concept as any play I've done before or since. I always say, if you get 51 percent of what you aim for, the production is a success. Certainly, this one came very near to what I wanted to do, which was to carry out Beckett's specific ideas. I have an old-fashioned idea, or maybe it's new-fashioned, that a director exists to serve the playwright and not to show off his own virtuosity. Every play I've done with a living playwright, I have tried to find out what he wanted, how he saw the play, and what his specific intentions were.

Since Beckett wouldn't come over for *Endgame*, I flew to Paris, even though I hate flying. There was a storm, and I thought we were going to crash. But I guess the trauma was worth it, to be able to discuss the play with Beckett at such great length before the rehearsals started.

This determination to do Beckett as he wanted it done led to an *Endgame* which I believe compares favorably with any of the five or six other productions I have seen of this play. We ran for about 110 performances, and we made a record album of the play. At last, Beckett was getting the kind of recognition he always deserved; he was becoming part of the bloodstream of American theater.

Wanting to continue working Off Broadway, I turned down more and more commercial comedies. The nominal salary I was getting drove my agent wild. Eventually, I stopped having an agent and still don't have one.

After *Endgame*, I did *The Summer of the Seventeenth Doll*, also in Greenwich Village. That play had been done on Broadway by the original Australian company and had received mixed reviews. I loved the play much more than the production. When I was offered the directing job, because I had staged it in Washington, I grabbed it. The cast was fine, the notices mostly good. The Off-Broadway revival ran about 150 performances, and we all had a great time working on it.

Finally, I was beginning to lose my image as the poor man's Josh Logan, and to be recognized with another cliché, that of an avant-garde director. Neither of these titles satisfied me. I don't like being labeled. I just wanted to do plays that I liked. My preferences have always leaned toward the unconventional. Even at college, I wrote my thesis on a little-known Russian playwright named Nicolai Evreinov who only now, years after his death, is being looked upon as a forerunner of the Theatre of the Absurd. In those days, that genre of theater didn't exist. But my taste for it did. To me, Kafka seemed the most revealing writer of the twentieth century, although Camus and Sartre became my favorites around World War II when I was coming into maturity. This, naturally led to my growing interest in Beckett.

When Sam gave me *Krapp's Last Tape* to read next, I immediately fell in love with it. This play had been preceded by *All That Fall*, a radio play which he wouldn't allow to be done on a stage. He wrote *Krapp* in English, instead of French as he usually does, and that gave it a somewhat different aura. Expressing himself in English first seems to alter Sam's tone. He becomes more compassionate and humorous and less cerebral. I was deeply touched by what might be called the "violin solo" of *Krapp's Last Tape*, whereas *Endgame* had appealed to me in a classical and cosmic manner as a block of granite. I remember when I first read *Endgame*, I felt as if it were a combination of *King Lear* and *Hamlet,* not to mention *Oedipus. Krapp*, in its more close-up human scale, moved me equally.

I knew that *Krapp's Last Tape* just had to be done Off Broadway. It took a long while to get it on, even though it was Beckett. At that time, those Off-Broadway coffeehouse productions were just starting, and Barney Rosset of Grove Press and I pursued the idea of doing the show in one of those places. I even considered putting it on at the well-known jazz club, the Five Spot. It would have been performed two or more times a night as a kind of solo nightclub act. Realizing, however, that the audience would be noisy, we then investigated a couple of other Village cafés that were quieter. Upon reconsideration, we were afraid that the tenuousness of the material might get lost in that atmosphere. So we decided to wait until we found another one-acter with which to present *Krapp* at an Off-Broadway house.

There was a lot of talk about a number of possible scripts. Then one day I heard about a play called *The Zoo Story*, by a young writer, Edward Albee, which had just been done in Berlin and which Sam also had known about. I read it and was overwhelmed with its powerful language and control. Unfortunately, it was not available for my direction; Edward had another director whom he knew.

I felt that *Zoo Story* was the most original and powerful American work that I'd read in years. There was no question about that. I've since directed it three times in its revivals at the Cherry Lane Theatre, although I can't take any credit for them because they were basically adaptations of the original, not only in terms of staging but also in concept. I found it very difficult to get away from the way it was first staged with George Maharis and Bill Daniels. In some respects my productions may have been better and in some respects not as good.

Sometimes, you know, I get credit for directing the play originally. I do my best to dispel this quaint notion, but not everyone believes me.

Getting together with an old friend of mine from Washington, Richard Barr, it was decided to present *Krapp*, and *Zoo* as a double bill. Of course, Sam had to approve of Edward's play, and Edward had to approve of Sam's, which he did because he had admired Beckett through the years. Sam also agreed to *Zoo* largely on our say-so.

My first impression of Edward Albee was that he was a very quiet, somewhat taciturn, sultry individual. I didn't have a great many conversations with him at the outset; he was not as easy to talk to then as he is now. I hardly got to know him at all during rehearsals, yet watching him I sensed there was below his surface calm a tremendous inner intensity, like molten lava. I longed to know more about him.

This production, my third away from uptown, made me feel completely at home and comfortable Off Broadway. I enjoyed every nickel of the twenty-five dollars a week I got for directing *Krapp's Last Tape*. This amount, however, was a little difficult to get along on, especially since my second child had just been born. To make a living, I had to travel around the country directing plays in various regional theaters, partly with the help of a Ford Foundation grant. My average for almost three years was one play a month. But I preferred that, hectic and peripatetic as it made my life, to unemployment insurance.

Simultaneous with directing *Krapp's Last Tape* in New York I was doing *The Cherry Orchard* in Washington. This required great understanding from producer Barr who, because he wanted me, was willing to put up with the logistic problems involved.

Donald Davis, who was cast as the original Krapp, was also most cooperative. Bringing a tape recorder with him, he came to Washington and stayed at Dick's mother's apartment. I would rehearse *The Cherry Orchard* until about five o'clock, meet Donald for dinner, and then rehearse from about seven until midnight with him, all by ourselves. There I was running through *Krapp's Last Tape* with its entire cast of one 250 miles off Broadway. Then the next morning it was *The Cherry Orchard* all over again.

Fortunately, Christmas and New Year's vacation at Arena Stage that year coincided with the previews of *Krapp's Last Tape*, giving me the freedom on days off to go to New York with Donald. Had the holidays fallen at any other time, I might not have been able to make this particular double play. As it was, things were quite hectic. And, once previews began, I had to commute between Washington and New York; with all the best intentions, of course, I had to miss some of them.

We opened at the Provincetown Playhouse, January 14, 1960, and as fate would have it, the occasion turned out quite well. We were worried because half the critics loved *Krapp* and hated *Zoo*, and half of them loved *Zoo* and hated *Krapp*. Somehow, we parlayed the mixed bag of notices into a hit. As a result, Dick Barr did something for me no other producer has ever done—he doubled my salary voluntarily, raising it from twenty-five dollars to fifty dollars a week.

Even though I had continued to work as a regional-theater director during this time, the productions of *Endgame*, *Seventeenth Doll*, and *Krapp* gave me a new image, that of being an Off-Broadway director. I liked working in this kind of less frenzied, more intimate, more stimulating theater. I still don't, however, like to be categorized as any one particular kind of director, Broadway, regional, or avant-garde. I am a director who, if he had to choose one place in New York to work in, would prefer Off Broadway.

Once becoming established in this league, I regretted not coming onto the scene earlier. I envied those of my colleagues who had more or less permanent roots, such as José Quintero and his Circle in the Square. Prior to this, I had not wanted to stay in New York/ Broadway depressed me. I didn't know how to survive in its rather rancid jungle. Moreover, I had no complete affiliation with any organization to which I could devote my talents. I once tried to get associated with Circle in the Square, but they didn't want me because I was competition. I was rebuffed in various other quarters, and I myself turned down a few possibilities, such as the Living Theatre, because they seemed a little kookier even than I was.

When I met Dick Barr and saw how he operated, I thought at first I'd like to join him as a producer, but then I realized I don't have the proper temperament for this/ I really didn't feel I was functioning properly unless I was directing. I didn't like doing plays just in a studio or loft. I didn't like looking for a job. I didn't like to sell myself, something I have never been able to do by explaining how I was going to stage a play. I just liked directing one play after another, and if people were impressed enough, they would come to me with other scripts.

That's exactly what happened as a result of *Krapp's Last Tape*. Edward got to watch me work; evidently he liked what he saw. Six months later, he called me up and asked me to do *The American Dream*. I was both delighted and touched by his offer, and looked forward to working with him and Richard Barr.

When we began rehearsals in November of 1960, I was completing an assignment to direct a play for the Actor's Workshop in San Francisco. Before I left New York, however, we had already finished casting *The American Dream*. I had to miss the first day of rehearsal because of the San Francisco opening and Edward was to take the actors for that one day.

I told him, "Please, just let the actors read the play and, for heaven's sake, don't discuss it or say anything special. Whatever you do, don't outline anything. Just tell them they're great and send them home."

Edward was fairly nervous and excited because this was his

first venture after *Zoo Story*. He agreed to do whatever I asked.

Upon my return to New York, Richard and Edward met me at the airport in a car. They both had exceedingly gloomy faces. I asked what the matter was, why the long looks? They told me that the actress who was playing Mommy had just quit.

"What do you mean, quit! She just started. What happened? Did she get another job?"

Edward said, "No."

"What did you do?" I insisted.

Edward told me, "We read the play, and I told them how great they were. Then they asked me some questions."

"And?"

"Well, I didn't say anything."

"Did you say anything to Mommy?"

Finally, Edward came out with it: "I told her that Mommy was a tumescent monster."

I could imagine exactly what happened. The actress went home after the rehearsal, and looked up "tumescent" in the dictionary. Finding out that it meant something horribly repellent, she quit. She didn't want to play anything tumescent, monster or otherwise. That demonstrates fairly clearly the danger of being unsubtly graphic with actors. I wouldn't have told the actress that Mommy was a "tumescent monster." I would have said that she should never listen to the other characters, that she should always talk louder than they, that she should treat them as though they did not exist; in effect, that mode of behavior would help to make her a tumescent monster.

The cast was rapidly reshuffled. Jane Hoffman, who was originally to play Miss Barker, became Mommy, much to her satisfaction and ours. In fact, I was pleased with the entire cast. After only eleven days' rehearsal, we opened at the York

Theatre on Sixty-fourth Street and First Avenue, a place that happened to be immediately available. Along with *The American Dream*, we presented an opera by Albee, his adaptation of Melville's *Bartleby* directed by another friend of Edward's who was familiar with the medium. The notices were good for the drama but, unfortunately, negative for the opera.

A short time afterward, I was in England working on *The Connection* when *Bartleby* was taken out of the bill, and it was decided that *The Death of Bessie Smith* would be its replacement. Because of my involvement abroad, I was not able to accept Edward's offer to direct it.

Before doing Edward's next play, *Who's Afraid of Virginia Woolf?*, I directed another of Beckett's masterpieces, *Happy Days*, with Ruth White and John C. Becher, at the Cherry Lane. (We were clobbered, and the play wasn't even faintly recognized as the major, marvelous, poetic work of art that it is, but we were all proud of it.) When we got to *Virginia Woolf*, I seriously recommended that it be done Off Broadway. I thought Broadway was not ready for it and that it wouldn't stand a chance commercially. At one time, we were going to do it simultaneously off and on Broadway. Then for various reasons and pressures, most of them having to do with expanding the audience for Edward's work, we wound up on the Main Stem. We worked on the play there exactly the same way we had done our Off-Broadway productions. And I worked very closely with the same group of people—the producing combine of Barr and Wilder, the stage manager and business manager, and indeed for the most part with actors whom I knew.

We huddled together for warmth against the theatrical elements. The author and producers gave us the psychological comfort and security that we needed. They gave us a set from the first day of rehearsal. They never impressed upon us the feeling that the play had to be a hit or that we were on a bigger stage now or that the stakes were greater, anything of that kind. Dedication to doing the work the best way possible was all that concerned us. At the most, we expected a kind of respectful reception, also that we would run two weeks. Of course, we didn't set out to be a failure, nobody does. But even if we thought we would get a run, we never anticipated two years out of it nor a Hollywood movie. What was most satisfying to me was that the production was an actual application of the Off-Broadway atmosphere and process that we had learned, and the informality and pleasantness that we had enjoyed there.

By now, I've done as many productions Off Broadway as on, and I have a definite viewpoint about the place of Off Broadway in our American theater. Originally, most of us came to it out of desperation, out of the need to find a place to work with some sanity, with some continuity, and with some fun. Broadway has stopped being that place because of the size of the investment and the absolute rigid need for success. The thing people don't realize about Off Broadway, which is critical, is that, in effect, it is a subsidized theater. It is subsidized by the people who work in it—the actors, the directors, and the playwrights, all of whom work for relatively nothing.

We talk about the opportunity to be discovered, to become a great star, or to make lots of money. Of course, this sometimes happens. But I never went to Off Broadway to be discovered; I had been discovered. I went there in order to work with better material under more creative conditions. I was subsidizing my opportunity to do that by being willing to work for twenty-five to fifty dollars a week. I think that often we forget that people do work Off Broadway not just to go on to something else but because the opportunities there, both artistically and personally, are more satisfying.

Lately, Off Broadway seems to be coming out of its morass of simply doing small Broadway or "showcase" productions. For a while, Off Broadway got just as slick and as contrived and as vulgarized as Broadway; it was doing things for either commerical gain or personal glory, to show off. To me, there's only one reason to work Off Broadway, and that is to create something worthwhile and individual. Not for financial profit, not to make a big splash, not to establish a reputation so that one can go to Sardi's for lunch. If and when this happens, it's not necessarily bad; but that certainly should not be the objective.

I didn't come to Off Broadway from purely altruistic motives. I don't think that good things in the theater come out of abstract ideals. As in the field of international relations, they come out of enlightened self-interest. We have to have a place in which to experiment, to work on plays with serious themes, plays that may have somewhat strange form or content, plays with limited audience appeal. We make allowance for specialized tastes in every other art but the theater. A book that is published and sells five thousand copies is still considered worth publishing, and is not looked down upon because it is not a half-million-copy best seller. Off Broadway is comparable to the highbrow paperback with its smaller audience and informal experience. (Interestingly enough *Waiting for Godot* has sold about seventy-five thousand copies so far, which is a fantastic amount for a play.)

I've often thought that our whole theater would be different if we had, earlier, the new Middle Theater five-hundred-seat houses, which can be a bridge between Off Broadway and Broadway. When there are a thousand seats and up, as on Broadway, everything is geared toward a certain economic return which makes it practically impossible for serious plays to have a chance. There aren't many people who want to see serious plays, and critics seem to be tougher on these works, so we wind up with a constant diet of musicals and comedies.

A Delicate Balance had a run of three and a half months, which is considered respectable but not commercially successful. Actually, it paid back its investment because Barr and Wilder happen to be especially astute producers.

Those in-between five-hundred-seat theaters, uninvolved as they are with Broadway production costs, will allow us to make a decent return on a product that wouldn't have to run a year or bring in eight thousand people a week. The people involved don't have to lower their economic sights as much as they would if they worked in a 199-seat Off-Broadway house. I'd be satisfied with attracting twenty-five hundred people a week. A book of poetry that sells that many copies in that time would be looked upon as a best seller. A play bringing in that number is fine for me, but too often the American theater suffers from putting too much emphasis on measuring success.

I hope that in the next decade the term "Off Broadway" will simply come to mean the nonprofit theater regardless of size, although I think that the proper size contributes something to the experience of viewing a play. In England, part of the great involvement with what's going on onstage is due to the intimacy of their playhouses, even their regular commercial West End theaters. It's exciting being close—hearing, sharing, and relating. When you do a play in a larger house, you're stuck with a completely different kind of experience. And now, with our usual blindness to what's real, though we're instituting the Middle Theater, we're headed more and more for building larger and larger theaters simply because we have to make enough money each week to support all those people behind the scenes as well as onstage.

We've got to get back to a human scale, to that sense of proportion and pleasure that one should have while working in the theater. And scaling down everything from production costs to ticket prices is vital. All the hoopla of buying seats six months in advance, spending thirty dollars, getting babysitters, parking the car, struggling with traffic, etc., have turned Broadway theatergoing into a real ordeal. Theatergoing must regain those personal qualities that Off Broadway began and still retains. After all, Off Broadway is only partly geographical and physical. Mostly it's psychological. It's a way of looking at the theater.

Regional theaters are national equivalents of Off Broadway.

Certainly, they're far enough off. The ones with which I am familiar don't tend to do Broadway hits; they do classics, slightly experimental or special works, or more literary-type plays. Also, the theaters are of necessity smaller in size. They offer a relief from the commercial ventures and psychology that predominates in New York. I think the regional-theater movement is a very healthy phenomenon, and I have high hopes for its future growth and development.

There are two kinds of theaters: those that present generally casual or popular entertainment, and those that are concerned with more serious and unusual material. The "boulevard plays," as the French call their more commercial entertain-ments, will always attract more people. Viña Delmar is always more popular than Dostoevski. Still, there must be room for both kinds of theater. This is true in literature, in music, in the visual arts, even in fashion or automobiles. We can't all ride great big luxury cars; some of us may actually prefer Volks-wagens.

Strangely enough, the regional theater sometimes stimulates the production of more far-out plays by other local groups. Typical of this is what's happening in Minneapolis as a result of the presence of the Guthrie theater. Like all interesting theater organizations, this one has its own special identity: doing the classics on an open stage with great style and gusto. The Guthrie theater exists not for profit but for social utility and good. The audience is educated to good taste as well as stimulated by the individual productions. As a result, smaller theaters have now sprung up, which are doing Beckett and Ionesco, playing the role of Off Broadway to the Broadway of the Guthrie theater.

Off Broadway now is not for the most part doing the job it once set out to do. There was a time when we were suddenly rediscovering Chekhov, Ibsen, Pirandello, and Brecht—all as a result of Off-Broadway productions. We had known these writers existed, but by seeing them onstage we found out that they could actually have meaning in today's world. We didn't mind that they didn't always pay off with high financial rewards. This sense of responsibility to the neglected masterpieces of dramatic imagination must be reestablished.

I have always enjoyed working Off Broadway, not only because it was more relaxing since the pressures and stakes were less, but also because the scale, which I think is so important, is more human. There are none of the gargantuan beasts battling on a cliff that are found on Broadway.

As for the expansion of my abilities, I could accomplish that anywhere I work, but I feel most creative in the Off-Broadway atmosphere. Since my success, I am not free to devote myself completely to that gratification. I'd find the time, however, if somebody would subsidize me with two hundred dollars a week, because I'd rather work Off Broadway than anyplace else.

VI
The Producer
and His Staff:
**THE PUBLIC
THEATRE**
All for All
The Producer:
JOSEPH PAPP

IN BROOKS Atkinson's review of my first Off-Broadway production, he told me to get out of the theater. I spent the afternoon on a bench in Central Park recovering. If anybody had told me that one day I would have my own theater in that park, I would have thought he was out of his mind. Who could imagine that such a crazy thing would actually happen—even to Brooks helping to make it possible!

Relentless self-appraisal of my motives and work helped me overcome that setback. I realized that I had some talent, but I had to learn how to cope with it. Before going into the Navy, I had worked at more than twenty odd jobs—from short-order cook to sheet-metal worker. The only reason I had gone into the theater is that I used to put on shows just for fun, and I decided to take it seriously.

As a poor ghetto kid in New York City, I was treated to a week of theater and opera by some charitable organization. I'll never forget seeing *Hamlet*.

When you're brought up with deprivation, you seek security, even if you want to be in the theater. I found my first theatrical home, after the war, in Hollywood at the Actors' Laboratory Theatre. It was made up of many of the people of the original Group Theatre who had come west to make their fortunes in film. In their free time they set up a school and theater. I trained there and became their manager until they were closed under political attack in 1950.

While I was at the Lab, Sarah Allgood, famous actress of the Abbey Theatre, appeared there in *Juno and the Paycock*. This production, as well as reading the autobiography of Sean O'Casey, excited me with that great playwright's use of language and view of life. Consequently, when I went back east, I wanted to do some of O'Casey's works. I wrote him and with the help of some Irish friends got an option on three of his one-act plays which had never been produced in New York.

My only previous experience in the city was with an amateur group which I directed when I first returned here. We had

Joseph Papp (Photograph by Benedict J. Fernandez)

put on *The Curious Savage* in a church at 729 East 6th Street, which, because of its Elizabethan atmosphere, was later to become the home of my first Shakespearean company.

My coproducers on the O'Casey plays were Peter Lawrence, who had presented Jean Arthur in *Peter Pan* on Broadway, and Bernard Gersten, who is now my associate producer. We managed to raise fifteen hundred dollars, but finding a theater was another matter. Finally, we got the Yugoslav-American Hall on 42nd Street, west of Ninth Avenue, where a lot of old revolutionaries would gather. With my limited background as a director, I was very much amazed at what went into doing a production. I worked on two of the one-acters, *Hall of Healing* and *Bedtime Story*. The third, *Time to Go*, was directed by Albert Lipton who had many credits.

Originally, I cast Lee Grant in one of the leads, but after a week of rehearsal, she left claiming that O'Casey was anti-woman. Anne Jackson replaced her. At that time she was as unknown as Lee Grant. Though the plays were set in Ireland and there were actual members of the Irish Republican Army in the cast, the lead in one of them was William Marshall, a black who assumed a brogue. There were also other blacks in smaller parts. This may have shocked people, but that was not the purpose. This kind of mixed casting is part of my approach. I find no discrepancy in it, having had an integrated upbringing. I simply choose the best actors available regardless of color.

After I was almost destroyed by Brooks Atkinson's review, the critic for another newspaper, *PM*, nominated *Bedtime Story* as the best play of the year. This reinforced my decision to stay in the theater, even though the show closed quickly. I was working at CBS, but I decided to experiment with Shakespeare at that church on East Sixth Street.

The place where I practice my craft must be like a home to me, so I tried to make one out of the basement there. My enthusiasm made my fellow workers at CBS help me. We in-

stalled the entire guts of a real playhouse. I nailed down seats
from an old movie house, helped rig up lighting, built parallels;
in fact, I was involved in every detail of converting the church
into a theater. Using my own hands to create that environment
gave greater inspiration to my directing. It seems my professional life always follows this pattern of building a theater
from scratch with the help of people who believe in what I
want to do.

I always loved Shakespeare's work. Even as a kid I memo-
rized huge sections of his plays. The language captivated me,
the sounds of the words and their dramatic quality. I wanted
to explore a more natural approach to Shakespearean speech. I
felt that actors were too loud and bombastic, and I wanted to
make it seem more real to more people. My intention was not
to minimize or throw away the lines, but to eliminate the
syrupy sounds American players imposed which took away
from the beauty of the emotion that is the soul of the poetry.

I realized those problems when I played Romeo at the
Actors Lab. Using the character-searching Stanislavsky method
which they endorsed there, the poetry seemed to get in the
way. I was obsessed with the idea of making the language
come out of the situation and so seem more real. My determination to bring new life to these words came from my fascination with the entire Elizabethan period as well as my adoration
of the plays.

Among my objectives was to make Shakespeare significant
to the contemporary scene, both artistically and socially. I also
wanted to provide a place where exceptionally talented people
could develop their powers; so many of our fine actors have
been destroyed by not doing the great parts. Equally important was to make these masterpieces available to the public
regardless of income; that is why we never charged admission.

To make that kind of theater possible, I spent more and
more time organizing and had to bring in other directors. At
the beginning we just experimented with scenes from

Shakespeare and Marlowe and did an evening of Shakespeare's women. Good actors were not hard to find, so many well-trained ones were out of work. Colleen Dewhurst had been knocking on doors for twelve years, then she starred in *The Taming of the Shrew* for me, and everyone asked, "Where've you been all this time?"

That appearance took place in the first season of Free Shakespeare in the Park which we presented at the East River Amphitheater on the Lower East Side of Manhattan in 1956, two and a half years after we began the Shakespeare Workshop. I found this old amphitheater on Grand Street near the East River. It was built by the WPA and had a band shell and two thousand seats. We went in there without getting a parks department permit, and despite the advice of the Neighborhood Association which warned against the constant holdups and stabbings. At first we couldn't get any critics to come down there. Finally, Arthur Gelb of *The New York Times* showed up. Even though he was rained out, he spoke so enthusiastically of the part of the play he saw to Brooks Atkinson that I was able to persuade that great critic, who once nearly wiped me out, to review us. He wrote a special Sunday piece on us that put us in business.

His praise helped me raise thirty thousand dollars from various foundations. Now we were able to begin our real operation. Prior to this, *The Taming of the Shrew* and *Julius Caesar* had cost us a total of five hundred dollars, including scenery and costumes. No one had been paid anything. We had gotten everything in every imaginative way possible. Now we had thirty thousand dollars to put on three productions, and I was able to pay my actors thirty dollars a week, which was the Off-Broadway minimum at that time. That in itself was an ambition fulfilled.

I was determined to have a mobile theater to take *Romeo and Juliet, Two Gentlemen of Verona*, and *Macbeth* all around New York. If people in Queens wouldn't come to Central Park to see Shakespeare, I would bring his plays to them. I wanted to have a truck with a stage on it, and one of my friends offered to build it for two thousand dollars. It turned out so rickety that the sanitation department had to haul it into the park one night. I got a permit the next day, and we played *Romeo and Juliet* for nearly three thousand people. I decided to continue with my plan to move this forty-five-foot platform trailer truck around the city. The strain of performing on this unit evenings and rehearsing on it during the day made it fall apart. I prevailed upon the parks department to allow me to set up shop in Central Park for the rest of the season. It was not until several years later that I was able to get a functioning mobile theater.

All our productions that summer were well received, but in the fall we were again faced with the problems of having neither money nor a home. I made connections within the mayor's office and got the department of welfare to allow us to use the Heckscher Theater on Fifth Avenue and 104th Street which was part of the facilities in a children's home. We fixed it over and presented *Richard III* with George C. Scott and *As You Like It*. Every night, after the performance, I'd make a pitch for money. I had become an expert on this. Although I had been stopped from doing it in Central Park, I managed to bypass the law by making my plea on the only corner that was not under the jurisdiction of the parks department. Somehow, we managed to survive with the few dollars we collected at each performance. Financial crises became our way of life, because we wanted to be an institution with continuity and charge no admission. We were the first free public theater in New York.

Our struggle with Robert Moses, who wanted to get us out of the park, focused public attention on us. When we won our battle in court, we got the city and George Delacorte to put up the $400,000 to build our permanent home in the park. Our summer productions in the park as well as the Spanish

Shakespearean unit, the mobile theater, and the children's theater occupied us from 1960 to 1966.

I had always wanted a permanent theater to do plays and operate year round. Though I was, and still am, constantly struggling for funds to present Shakespeare, I still desired an outlet for shows that had concern for what was happening in the contemporary world. For a couple of years I was on the lookout for just such a place. Of course, I didn't have the money, yet I believed that if I found such a building, I would be able to finance it.

After a couple of years of looking, I came across the Astor Library in Greenwich Village. It was a shambles, but I saw its potential to fulfill our requirements. Then I found out it had been already sold and was going to be torn down in six months to make way for a high-rise apartment building; I persuaded the city to declare the building a landmark, and confronted the new owner. After much dickering I convinced him that he owed the city some recompense for his affluence, and he agreed to sell the building to us. The building cost over a half million dollars, and we still owe more than half of that amount.

We have already put over a million dollars into renovation. Because we are so in love with the Italian renaissance structure, we are intent on preserving the original design features and incorporating them into our concept of theater. So far we have two theaters of 299 seats each, and one experimental theater of a hundred seats in the basement, where we can try out plays before bringing them upstairs.

Now that I had a place to present plays, the question was what contemporary plays would be appealing to the general audience I wanted to attract. Beckett and Pinter-type works were too special. I was thinking of opening with a play by John Arden, the Englishman who writes so skillfully, but then I had qualms about it since I thought I should open this new theater with a play by an American.

One night, on my way back from Yale where I was teaching, Jerome Ragni sat in the next seat to me on the train. We talked about *Viet Rock* which we had both just seen, and then he said, "I've just written something with Jimmy Rado. Would you like to see it?" I said, "What is it?"

"Well, it's kind of a musical called *Hair.*" He then showed me six or eight handwritten pages. I read it and asked, "Do you have any more?"

"There are more pages at home," he answered. I told him to bring them to me in the morning and that I would read them. On going through the rest of *Hair,* without the music, my reaction was that it wandered all over the place, some of it was boring and some interesting. The thing that struck me was that it had to do with the loneliness of young people, and that's why I became involved in the material. Galt MacDermot was brought in to write the music, and I decided to do it with Gerald Freedman, who had directed our Shakespearean productions.

Everybody thought I was crazy to open up the Public Theatre with an untried hippie musical, particularly since our traditional background had not prepared us for such a production—but *Hair* went on to make theatrical history.

Out of the four productions we did the first season, none of them came directly from an agent. I adapted a modern *Hamlet* myself, I kept after a particular writer to write a play, and I met someone who knew about a unique work. It set up a pattern which, I feel, is the way the Public Theatre should operate. We would have to get our own plays—some way. Our first season cost us $300,000, and we considered it quite successful. Our next year, everything we did was much more subjective and didn't go over too well.

Our agreement with playwrights is that their plays run eight weeks, and they are guaranteed $2,500 against 6 percent of the gross. With our low price structure, we require an annual Public Theatre subsidy of $750,000. We believe in maintaining

The original production of *Hair* at the Public Theatre (Photograph by George E. Joseph)

a creative staff all the time, so that we are prepared to mount what we believe in almost at a moment's notice. This continuity of employment not only gives us loyalty but also allows us to have top people at lower guaranteed salaries. Each of us knows what we can expect of each other and that contributes to our own particular style as a group.

Theoni V. Aldredge, Ming Cho Lee, and Martin Aronstein, have a permanent home here, but they also have to work outside to maintain themselves. We have a prop department, a wardrobe department, and facilities to make our own sets. We also have permanent lighting maintenance and a technical director. We pay more and we get more. Even our actors average twice as much as the Off-Broadway minimum.

Our basement theater was run by a young director who was a student of mine at Yale, Ted Cornell. He was given $25,000 to do an entire season of four to six plays. Each runs three weekend performances, and the writer gets a hundred dollars, unlike most showcases where he gets nothing. The actors also get a hundred dollars for the whole run. Keeping the costs so minimal makes us freer to do more daring plays. Though we don't have a writer's workshop, the writer works with the director in developing the material.

We base our choice of plays on what we consider a distinguished idea expressed through first-rate writing. A play must also be meaningful, not in the political or social sense, but in a point of view that is very strong. We have no use for the usual Broadway comedy, and I wouldn't do a play in blank verse because of my involvement with Shakespeare. We always are on the lookout for plays that will attract three hundred people to each performance. The audience I most prefer would consist of students, intellectuals, and people off the street. The Broadway audience might be very nice people as individuals, but I wouldn't want to do plays for them as a group. I like to do shows that have something to say in a beautiful, interesting, or challenging way. I want the ideas of the play to engage me, so that I learn something from it. If the play doesn't instruct me, I'm not interested in it. I don't want to hear just arguments on stage, but good strong confrontations are fascinating. That's why trial plays and dramatizations of ideas that we are concerned about now are so marvelous. When you come into the theater, you should be guaranteed that it will be more than life. It should extend what you get in the newspapers and on TV—otherwise why go?

We're always searching for new plays. We read well over a thousand scripts a year and have set up a complete play-reading apparatus. We also invite new directors that we hear about to come in on our experimental productions and to assist our regular director.

Our biggest dramatic hit to date, *No Place to Be Somebody*, came from a black man who knew the author, Charles Gordone, and asked Ted to read it. He liked it, and I also agreed that it was a worthwhile script that we should try working on for the Other Stage. By the second week of rehearsal, it showed a lot more possibilities than we had imagined. The text was deceptive, having much more life than it had indicated. At the first preview it seemed very long, but I knew that this play was going to be something. Before that opening I had told the company that we were going to turn it into a full Equity show and take it upstairs. I immediately put them on regular upstairs salary even though we had to run it for six more weeks before that theater was available.

Critical acclaim brought full houses, as well as a chance to continue this play in a regular Off-Broadway run and to present it in other countries. We are also going to make a film of the show. The Pulitzer Prize is its crowning achievement—especially since Charles Gordone is the first black playwright to receive that award—and for an Off-Broadway production, too!

Just to operate our building alone costs us $100,000 a year. The average production costs $65,000 per play to mount and run, and that includes the building deficit. We offer unusual plays at low prices amidst glamorous surroundings that are comfortable—even for the actors backstage. We have two three-hundred-seat theaters, the Anspacher and Estelle R. Newman, the first on the second floor in the former main reading room of the Astor Library—a thrust-stage, wrap-around-audience theater that is handsome, intimate, and flexible. The second theater is located in a chamber created out of the basement—next to our hundred-seat experimental theater—and ground floor of the south building, an end-arena, platform stage facing a steeply banked, single, solid phalanx of audience—starkly modern and virtually a workshop for the making of plays. Just beyond the main-floor lobby will be a very informal theater featuring free-style seating and a stage that shifts from full arena to platform-proscenium, seating between 125 and 150 people and which will serve as a children's theater weekends and holidays and as a coffeehouse theater throughout the year. A chamber recital hall accommodating 150 people will be created on the third floor of the south wing for concerts, play readings, and poetry recitals. A magnificent rehearsal hall will be on the third floor, north wing, which will serve all festival productions.

Our entire involvement with the arts and the public resulted in a black arts gallery and a photographic workshop for thirty black and Puerto Rican children. On Saturday nights we have midnight concerts where five hundred people lie on the floor listening to all kinds of music. Another medium we're into is films—exhibiting and producing. We've incorporated a small movie house which shows avant-garde and important archive films in a unique environment that isolates the viewer.

I know that the underlying philosophy of financing is relatively simple: the value of the theater to its community will serve to guarantee its economic viability. The fact that I owe over a million dollars, however, keeps me awake nights.

Theoni V. Aldredge

The Costume Designer:
THEONI V. ALDREDGE

WHEN I was a sixteen-year-old schoolgirl in Greece, I went to see a film called *Caesar and Cleopatra*. The clothes were so extraordinary and made the star, Vivien Leigh, look so spectacular that I decided to build a career for myself as a theatrical costume designer. I had three things working for me: a love for the theater, a flair for design, and a belief, common to most young people, that anything I decided to do was supremely possible.

A search for a theater school with a good design department led me to the Goodman Memorial Theatre School of the Art Institute of Chicago. After three years of study, I was awarded a fellowship by which I continued at Goodman for two more years as head of their costume-design department. Those years at Goodman were a time of total immersion into every aspect of the theater: history, theory, play analysis, scene design, lighting design, costume design, sketching, color, draping—even directing and a bit of acting.

There is only one thing my training did not prepare me for—the Big Time Broadway Producer with half a million dollars of someone else's money riding on a shaky vehicle and whose wife and/or girlfriend and/or secretary thinks she knows more about costuming than the entire membership of the United Scenic Artists and the Designers' Guild en masse. And when panic sets in (and on Broadway, opening is commonly referred to as "panic time"), everybody stand back! The actor ("Fire the maid!"), the playwright ("Give me two new acts by sundown!"), the scenic designer ("Instead of a Bronx kitchen, it now takes place on the beach at Brighton!"), and the costume designer ("Put everybody in pink sequins!") are in for agony. I have found in more than a few instances that, when the curtain goes up on one of my Broadway opening nights, I sit there criticizing the costumes as though they had been done by someone else, because in fact they have.

I want to be responsible for my own mistakes not someone else's, just as I want the costumes to represent my own skill and talents, not some intruder's whimsy. But after over seventy Broadway shows, I realize that Broadway is not the Theater, but merely a theater—a rather sickly arena where individual genius is rather less appreciated than conglomerate overkill designed to dazzle that one newspaper critic who means the difference between financial success and ruin.

There is another theater, however—Off Broadway—whose values and priorities (until recently anyway) have been a great deal more qualitative. I started Off Broadway, I still work there, and if economics would permit, I would gladly stay there.

After a season with the Studebaker Repertory Theatre in Chicago, I came to New York armed with a pitiful portfolio of school sketches and an abundance of blessedly naïve enthusiasm. A year later I still had the former but much less of the latter. "When you do something, let me know!" was the usual response at the interviews I managed to get.

Finally I met a producer who was doing *Heloise* Off Broadway. In the fifties, Off Broadway was still looked upon as a showcase, much as Off Off Broadway is regarded today. I showed him my portfolio, told him that I could cut, drape, and sew as well, and was delighted to be hired at $150 for four weeks' work. It was a period play, and the budget was an extravagant $250. I made the costumes on the floor of my living room, using drapes, sheets, tablecloths, any piece of fabric I could lay my hands on. I tinted, dyed, painted, aged, and used every resource at my command (which didn't include money) to get the look I wanted. In the end everyone was pleased—most importantly myself.

Then one of those impossible dreams came true. Geraldine Page, for whom I had designed at the Studebaker Theatre, asked me to design her costumes for Williams' *Sweet Bird of Youth* on Broadway. I never stopped working after that.

I started switching then between Broadway and Off Broadway, and began to sense the peculiar differences. Economically, of course, the dissimilarity is obvious—one provides a living wage, the other does not. But the most important variance is one of trust and confidence and artistic emphasis, best illustrated by the fact that Off Broadway I find myself dealing mostly with the director and actors, while on Broadway I waste a good part of every day trying to avoid the company's sweaty-palmed business manager. Off Broadway, if a certain design can't be afforded, you change the entire design to something within the budget, but on Broadway the company will accept the design for, say, a six-hundred-dollar costume and then attempt to save the money by cutting a sixty-cent flower or a two-dollar fringe. The economy is ridiculous, of course, and by the time they've finished nibbling away at your work you have a chronic headache to match their fearful foolishness. I'm speaking generally, of course. There are notable exceptions both on and off, but that stamp of originality that marks a designer's work as his own is less likely to become obliterated Off Broadway.

This is particularly true at the New York Shakespeare Festival. Once producer-director Joseph Papp has selected a play, his entire organization will stretch every capacity to give that play the richest mounting possible. He treats people the same way; once having chosen you, his faith in you is boundless. Even when you make a mistake (and who doesn't eventually?), it's a mistake shared in common among equals. Such a working atmosphere is pure luxury. It allows one to stretch and grow and occasionally to be brilliant. When I first arrived in New York, I showed my work to Mr. Papp, but it took Gerald Freedman joining the staff the following summer to get me the job. Gerry and I met while working on a Hasty Pudding show at Harvard. I've been Joe's resident designer ever since. We never have enough money, but somehow Joe never talks about it. When there's something we need, we just get it.

One day Joe called us all down to show us a building he was about to buy. I thought he was crazy, because it was crumbling, but he had fantastic plans for it. What I took for insanity turned out to be great foresight. The Astor Library is an ideal place to work in. We have our own workrooms where we produce our clothes much cheaper. We took a chance, but it worked out well. My shopmaster, Milo Morrow, interprets sketches like a magician. He knows fabric and line, and has unlimited patience. We started with a box of pins that cost fifty-five cents, two sewing machines, and a couple of dummies. Somehow, we pulled through that first summer. From then on, it worked marvelously. Young people, interested in working Off Broadway, came in as apprentices, learning their craft. We complain about youth all the time; they're not good for this or that, and they do ugly things. The youngsters who are with us are of school age, between seventeen and twenty, and they come to work all summer for very little money, just for an on-the-job education. We teach them how to make armor, to paint clothes, to cut as well as to sew. There are usually about twenty people under the guidance of Milo, and we get great satisfaction from watching them grow. The first year they have very little to do beyond a hem or a hook and eye. The next season they begin to cut and assemble clothes. How great it is to see how hard these young people are willing to work.

In the winter we have a much smaller crew. Milo, of course, stays on with his two assistants, and we hire according to the needs of the show, even with the big ones rarely more than two or three. A great economy comes from the fact that the Public Theatre owns all the clothes we make, and we can reuse them again and again. Our stock of Shakespearean costumes are the best ever because they are built like real clothes.

I get jobs mostly through my agent who submits me to producers, but often people hear about me, or an actor or director wants me particularly. I especially like working Off Broadway because there people still have their wits about them. You read the script, then turn to your director for a real

good, old-time discussion of characters, what makes them the way they are, and what they are doing in the play. That comes first, not like on Broadway, where they just ask you how much it's going to cost. I find talking to my actors, too, important, because there are certain things that they are going to do onstage, maybe moving a specific way, and they might require a special costume to help them. Discussions with the scene designer are also very important, because I have to know which way he's going so that I can imagine the clothes within the environment. I also have to know about the lighting. After I've gotten the facts, I sit down and draw very rough sketches which I show to my director to make sure I'm on the right track. I let the actors see them to find out their feelings. Then I choose colors; I have an absolute passion about colors because I see them talking, they have something to say. There are a hundred details, from the final sketch to the actual making of the costumes, in which the love of my work, I hope, shows.

The Off-Broadway minimum is $350 plus a small royalty that's like the management rewarding you for your help in making the show a success. In a big show on Broadway you get paid by the costume: seventy-five dollars for the leads and supporting actors, and fifty dollars extras; also, you get twenty-five dollars for repeats, variations of a particular costume for a whole crowd.

It's not unusual for a contemporary show to use store-bought clothes, but I don't like it. I don't think that people onstage should look like people in life; they're just a bit bigger and should be treated that way. I simply won't use that kind of costume anymore. I feel I'm beyond that.

I fight for my integrity. I have to, because my actors have to be happy. When the chips are down, I'm not on that stage, neither is the producer. You can have theater without clothes, like it or not, but you can't have a show without an actor.

To get started, a costumer should find out how the machinery works. Besides what talent you might have, you

Preliminary sketch by Theoni Aldredge for Rose in Act Two of the Public Theatre's production of *Trelawney of the Wells* should learn the technical aspects by apprenticing with a designer. Until you're in the union, you can work as a second assistant where, though no designing is involved, you're at least around to see how fittings are conducted, fabrics and accessories are chosen, and details are checked out. A professional shop is your best school.

When I work Off Broadway, it's as a working designer who is infatuated with a property or the style of a director. People are kinder there. Once in a while you find somebody decent on Broadway. I must say that if I could make my living Off Broadway, that's where I'd stay.

The Set Designer:
MING CHO LEE

Ming Cho Lee
(Photograph by Robert D. O'Connor)

THERE ARE very few American set designers who are
fortunate enough to have codesigned the theaters they work in
and who have a permanent relationship with a continuing
producing institution. It's good to know that you have a constant source of activity as well as a chance to develop within a
framework of people to whose talents you relate.

This ideal situation came about in 1962 when Joseph Papp
saw my work for Martha Graham and was in need of a set
designer; at that time there was very little status and pay for
the job. That was the year we opened the Delacorte Theater
and I did three productions, and I've been his principal scenic
designer ever since.

Off Broadway gave me my first chance to be entirely responsible for designing a production. After five years as an assistant to other scenic designers such as Jo Mielziner, I was hired by the Phoenix Theatre to do *The Infernal Machine* starring June Havoc. Herbert Berghof, the director, and I didn't get along because I was stubborn and inexperienced. Our differences were compounded when Brooks Atkinson, who didn't like the show, gave the set a good notice.

My next experience, Off Broadway, was equally unhappy. Word Baker had a marvelous production idea for *The Crucible*. It was to be very nonliteral. We took it to Arthur Miller with a model of the set, and we won his approval to go ahead with the production. We were to do it at the Carnegie Playhouse, but it was too expensive. Instead, we wound up at the Hotel Martinique. This changed the concept from a thrust-stage to an arena-stage presentation. Then we ran out of money, and I had to put half of my four-hundred-dollar fee back into the show. Finally all the sets were eliminated, and we wound up with a carpet and some props.

That setback is not unusual for Off Broadway. Money is often a problem, but just as important for a set designer is the fact that you can't really prepare for your job properly until the theater is assured. Every house is different; one may have a thrust stage, another may be a little room with an eight-foot ceiling and a stage at the end, or there are a dozen other variations you can't anticipate. Usually you don't know what specific problems you're going to encounter until two weeks before rehearsal. That's why working for the Public Theatre and the Shakespeare Festival has been a relief.

Off-Broadway producers can be just as unscrupulous as Broadway producers. They often want you to do everything, including painting the set. I get very tired of people saying that you can use your imagination and design with one penny. I don't believe in having a lot of money and wasting it, and certainly working with Joe Papp, I know how to be conservative about expenses, but often you spend all your thinking on how to use that one penny and wind up designing nothing. Every time, it seems, that I work Off Broadway, I feel the responsibility of fulfilling my ideas so much that I take money out of my own pocket—that makes me a little wary. Yet, I don't consider myself a Broadway designer, since I only do on the average of one musical a year.

I know that, if you don't have money, you must make do, but I believe that only permanent institutions should be allowed that privilege. That's why I particularly enjoy the Public Theatre and my other jobs with the City Opera, The Juilliard School of Music, and the American Opera Center.

My approach to a show at the Public Theatre, after reading the script, is to question the director about an overall production scheme, discussing the choices of whether to be realistic or abstract, should it be in the period or way out, and what should the material of the set be—metal, wood, granite, or whatever? Then I do a very rough sketch that's just clear enough to show the director and find out whether I'm going in the right direction. Afterward, I make a small model in one-eighth scale. Eventually, I work it up to a one-half-inch scale model and paint it up. When this is approved by Joe Papp and the director, we draft the working designer's elevation and other detailed specifications which we send to a shop. Here, again, we have another advantage in being an institution. Unlike the usual Off-Broadway condition, in which you run around to find a person who can build your set in his garage, we have a scenery studio of our own at the Public Theatre, and for the Delacorte productions we use an outside shop that has always built our sets, and it's one of the largest and most skillful in town, Pete Feller. He takes a lot of burden off my back. A designer is often called upon to do physical labor when he works Off Broadway, because once you get a set from a shop and they put it in, you are expected to put in the finishing touches yourself, since you don't have a production carpenter.

It may seem romantic to work Off Broadway, but, believe me, it's rough when you see ideas disappear before your eyes, and you are required to do physical labor that is not quite your responsibility, but it's either you or it won't get done. The pay isn't that great either. It used to be a ridiculous minimum of $128, now it's been increased to an impossible $220 plus a percentage that adds up to about a dollar a performance. You might say that the scene designer helps subsidize Off Broadway.

Though the Shakespeare Festival is a 100-percent-deficit organization, they at least try to give better working conditions and pay people fairly. Joe now pays me only slightly less than Broadway minimum for a one-setter. Of course, the productions at the Delacorte are much more complicated than that, but it's a respectable fee. During the summer I have a staff of two or three who help me put the shows on and are paid by Joe.

My basic concept for designing outdoors is never to compete with the natural elements. I'm very careful about using foliage at the Delacorte, because you just can't beat the real thing that surrounds you. With the Belvedere Tower in the background, I'm also cautious about using realistic architecture in a similar shape onstage, because the tower would dwarf anything I could do and would make it seem unbelievable. I don't think you should mask everything in trying to create an intimate stage, or to cut the outdoors out; after all, you are in the open air. I never design pictorially for this kind of thrust stage.

Under those conditions, I always try to set up a formal framework where realistic elements, or what I call selective realities, are somehow put within a formal abstract framework. Essentially the concept is to make a statement compatible with the play and to create a total environment. It's a nonliteral approach that is right for Shakespeare; the Globe itself was a presentational place. My consciousness of that has in-

Ming Cho Lee's set for *Ergo* at the Public Theatre (Photograph by Nathan Rabin)

fluenced my design. Since the audience is on three sides, my sets are more sculptural, and since everything outdoors is three-dimensional, I deal with space and volume. After working on almost thirty productions at the Delacorte, I'm totally convinced of these theories.

As for the Public Theatre, I get paid slightly less than for the Delacorte, and I take care of my assistants. The productions are simpler than those at the park. I can hardly think of any Off-Broadway theater that can compete with our working conditions. Besides having the environment of a beautiful building, there are clean dressing rooms and showers. When I did the production of *Othello* at the Martinique for Ted Mann, I confirmed my impression of how horrible most of those theaters are. You change in the basement, work till three o'clock in the morning, and there's always a greasy smell that's unbelievable.

For the Anspacher Theatre, I pretty much design nonpictorially, too. Right now, I feel that the theater dictates a certain kind of style that has more height than width, and so the total visual impact is vertical, unlike other theaters where the ceiling is low. It's also a nonliteral theater and cannot be pictorial. The approach must be formal, because in the middle of the stage there are two columns that proclaim the space. These factors totally influence the design.

As for the Estelle Newman Theatre, it requires another style because the grid comes from the stage all the way into the audience, and creates a feeling that the actors and the audience are in the same room. Most Off-Broadway theaters that have this kind of layout profit by the feeling of intimacy, unlike Broadway houses that have picture-frame separation. There's more involvement when all the people are under one roof. This is true in the park, as well, with the sky as the ceiling.

Working under any condition Off Broadway does give you a chance to get started. As it turns out, I have not strayed far from that milieu myself—but then with such a setup, who would want to?

Martin Aronstein (Photograph by Robert D. O'Connor)

The Lighting Designer:
MARTIN ARONSTEIN

IN THE summer of 1957 the New York Shakespeare
Festival's mobile theater was playing *Romeo and Juliet* in
King's Park near my home in Queens. I joined the company by
wandering into the site and asking the lighting designer, John
Robertson, if he needed help. He gave me a tired answer, because he was terribly overworked and had been bothered previously by other people who had made similar offers and never
followed through. "Yeah, I need help," he said. "Show up
tomorrow morning."

Anxious for the opportunity, because I had become interested in lighting while I was in Queen's College, I asked, "What
time tomorrow?"

"As soon as your mother will let you out of the house."

When I arrived at eight, I thought I'd be the first one on the
job, but John was already there, sleeping—catching a few hours'
nap after having worked all night. I immediately became an
apprentice and have been with the Shakespeare Festival ever
since, taking over as lighting designer when John Robertson
died a few years ago. All the while I've been working on and
Off Broadway, as well.

My approach to lighting may be a little different than that
of others, but basically, I'm sure we all begin the same way. I
read the script for content. Then I go through it again very
carefully, breaking it down, scene by scene and moment by
moment, with the playwright's direction first. If the playwright says that in act one sunlight is streaming through the
window, and in act two moonlight is shining, I know, therefore, that I need sunlight and moonlight and lighting in the
room that is motivated by sunlight and moonlight, such as
artificial, practical lamps onstage. Then, there are a series of
meetings with the director and set designer. Depending upon
the complexity of the show, the set designer will consult with
me about such factors as what material to use for backdrops
and how they are to be treated in terms of lighting—before the
designs are even set. Very often we will talk about the hanging

of the show, where the scenery hangs from the lines, from the grid, from the area above the stage where it is suspended in space. Naturally, there has to be room for lighting equipment overhead, as well as for the scenery to be in the proper place when it is lowered onto the stage.

I really learned lighting Off Broadway, mostly at the Shakespeare Festival, but also at the Equity Library Theatre where I did ten productions in eight months. Unlike Broadway, the designer does the physical labor himself and really gets a feeling for the basics. He does not simply direct others to do the focusing: he does it himself and in that way gets to know every instrument. There is also the chance to experiment with individual moments, because you are not pressured by time or money. The labor may be unskilled and the personal physical strain may be greater, but so is the personal satisfaction of total involvement.

In *Dames at Sea*, which I lit Off Broadway, there was one switchboard operator and one follow-spot man, neither of which had to be union members; usually people who like to hang around the theater and do odd jobs get involved with this end of the production. When I did *Promises, Promises* on Broadway, we had three switchboard operators, three follow-spot operators, and one man who handled the electric motors —all union members.

Often when I work Off Broadway, I can come in after midnight, when all the actors have left, and set up. This allows me to do several productions at a time. The typical fee for an Off-Broadway straight play is about $200, and includes the complete laying out of the show, which with meetings, viewings, thinking, and working may take the better part of a week. From then on there is the actual handling of the show which the lighting designer must supervise personally, and that can take three or four days. He is also responsible for running dress rehearsals, the technical rehearsals, attending previews, all in addition to the setting up of the lights. Often this can take as much time as a Broadway production where the minimum is $1,250. There is also royalty, in both cases, in which the lighting designer shares.

I not only designed the permanent lighting setups for the Public Theatre, but also I'm basically responsible for the lighting of each show. I suspect I'm the only lighting designer who has a permanent, full-time associate, Lawrence Metzler. The usual workday for setting up a show is about fifteen hours.

Working Off Broadway is like going back to the sources. Everybody is so excited about a production, and they are willing to do new things. If that different bit doesn't work out, there is no great catastrophe, because not much money was spent. It's fun to take chances, and often it pays off. Theoni V. Aldredge, Ming Cho Lee, and I feel that at the Public Theatre we can extend ourselves without worrying about making a mistake.

One of the most exciting projects I've worked was for the New York Shakespeare Festival mobile theater. Because we play one-night stands outdoors, with no time to focus lights since you need darkness for that, we have perfected a prefocus situation, where we roll out towers that elevate hydraulically, and project lights that have been preset at a nighttime rehearsal. All this has been measured very carefully, so that the lights can be reproduced anywhere accurately.

Unlike Broadway, where you rent all of your lighting equipment, most Off-Broadway theaters have permanent installations. The pipes which provide the hooking are better than the balcony rail which are flat dead front on Broadway, where they are concerned about marring the beauty of the house. Off-Broadway lighting equipment hanging in the middle of the ceiling is part of the whole theatrical experience and is quite valuable as a positive addition to the environment. Generally, I don't think the audience pays too much attention to lighting equipment once something interesting is happening onstage.

In the course I teach at Columbia, I cover the technical

aspects of lighting and also try to instill the ability to com-
municate ideas in terms of lighting, so that the director and
the lighting designer can talk about specific problems with
each other. Too often directors come into productions saying,
"I don't know, the lighting is too bright, it's too blue, or it's
too green." I hope the day will come when a director will be
able to say in clear terms like this, "For this scene, could we
have a little bit less dead front light, and a little more side light
and back light," or, "I don't think the true colors of the costumes are coming out with that blue. Could we add some
warm color—lavender or something that might pick up and
enhance the complexion of the actor, if possible?"

Those who want to be lighting designers should realize that,
though it looks easy, it's not—and you can't get rich doing it,
either. The technical aspects of lighting can be learned at
school, but the best way to become a lighting designer is to go
and work anywhere you can get a job. When I did all that
work for the Equity Library Theatre, I wasn't paid, but it was
a chance to get experience when no one else would use me. A
situation like that leads to contacts. A person who appreciates
your work passes your name on to someone else, and that's
how it can all begin.

VII
The Actress:
COLLEEN DEWHURST
Of My Own Free Will!

UNLIKE MOST young girls, I was not interested in becoming an actress when I was little. In fact, acting was the furthest thing from my mind. Being very much of a tomboy, I wanted to be an aviatrix. Since I was also interested in writing, my mother said that, if I would go to college for two years, she would let me take up flying. In my senior year in a Milwaukee high school—one of the fifteen schools I went to from the time we moved down from Montreal—all that changed.

An English teacher was casting *As You Like It* according to the way he felt the characters should look. He wanted me to play Olivia. By coincidence my first role was in Shakespeare, and twelve years later my big break came from playing Kate in *The Taming of the Shrew*. The only reason I endured the agony of going on that first time was that it was a requirement of passing my speech course. All that I remember of the show was that, when it came time to itemize the beautiful qualities of my features, my veil got caught, and it brought the house down.

Later, as a freshman at Milwaukee Downer College for Young Ladies, I put on a skit for my class because I hated what another young girl was trying to do. By then, I liked what I did so much that I wanted to become an actress.

When I told my mother that I'd changed my mind and wanted to go to acting school in New York, she said, if she could see me do something, she would decide. She felt that mediocrity had no place in the arts, and if she thought I would just be ordinary, she would insist that I give up my ambition at once.

One of my best friends had written a play on Pasteur, and I wanted to play the lady who pleads with him to give her son the serum before it had been perfected. This took some convincing since I had a reputation for being the class clown. Rehearsals were impossible for me because I was so self-conscious and embarrassed. Opening night I virtually went

Colleen Dewhurst (Zodiac Photographers)

on cold. After the performance, I went home with my mother, and we sat down in the living room without turning on the lights. I was overwhelmed when she said it was all right for me to go to drama school.

For my audition at the American Academy of Dramatic Art in New York, I wrote my own material, not knowing that everyone normally did well-known scenes. Mine was a depressing sketch about a woman whose furniture was laughing at her. When they accepted me, I thought it was so marvelous—not realizing at the time that they would have accepted a tree if it had applied.

Even though I was leaving at the end of the second year, the president of the college wrote a letter to my mother saying that, if I hadn't resigned, she would have dismissed me because she felt that I had no sense of responsibility. My mother, who was a very strong lady, agreed, and I was enraged when she insisted that I spend a year going to work to find out what it was like to earn my own living.

This was near the end of World War II, and I went to stay with a friend in Gary, Indiana, to try to get work in a defense plant, since I had no secretarial skills. I was refused by every one of those factories because I was an alien from Canada, which got me so mad that I would scream, "If we're good enough to fight with, we're good enough to work with." I ended up running an elevator, and I was so bad at it that I never hit the floors. One day I had a toothache when a dentist who was riding in the elevator became interested in me and I wound up as his receptionist.

At the end of that year of work, I had a more serious attitude, and I never missed a day at the academy. Since then, I realize that the only area of my life in which I have complete discipline is the theater. I take great pride in that and never miss a performance. I'm always on time, and I'll probably study acting the rest of my life.

While at the academy I married a handsome and talented actor, James Vickery. On my graduation from this place, which I consider to be like a finishing school, an instructor gave me a job as a leading lady in a new stock company in Knoxville, Tennessee, for thirty-five dollars a week—an incredible sum. I felt the world was mine.

I was introduced to that very conservative community in *Personal Appearance* playing a shady actress who tries to seduce a young hick. After the show, people from the audience would bring cake and gifts to everyone in the cast but me. They wouldn't even speak to me. When the reviews came out I wasn't even mentioned, although I played the leading role, until the end, with "Colleen Dewhurst looked the part." They actually thought I was the character I was playing and refused to laugh at anything I would do and just loathed me because I was a villainess. "Coat of armor, my dear," the director would tell me, "coat of armor!"

In our next production I was a wisecracking woman, and to play it safe they removed all the blasphemy from my part. One night a prop wouldn't work, and I let out with "Well, I'll be a son of a bitch!" and the house fell in. To this day I can't understand it, because after that I was their love.

Following that job, I came back to New York and the pattern of my life for the next ten years was only to be in summer stock while working at odd jobs in the winter. For three years I had a very good job as an usher at Carnegie Hall. Then I was a gym girl at a reducing salon, putting the ladies through their exercises. I also worked for the phone company as a free-lance switchboard operator. That one was great because we got our ten dollars at the end of the day and I could go home and eat.

I was also taking classes with Joseph Kramm and Joseph Anthony at the American Theatre Wing. This was the time when the Method was really taking over, and it seemed like we would be eternal students. One day Joe Kramm said, "Ladies and gentlemen, you must get out on the streets and look for work. You cannot keep coming to classes and not working because this isn't what the theater is all about." Though we realized what he said was true, we kept on studying because it made us feel safe while we were starving.

Money was always a problem, even while I was working in stock. There were companies that folded, and once I had a fight with the local sheriff because I was overseeing the cashbox to make sure the actors got paid. He had come to claim the money, and I was wrestling with him until a couple of actors came to my rescue. Ten years of stock, and you feel it's a way of life come summer. Now, of course, I'm in a position where I'm not supposed to accept that kind of job, and besides the type of stock that did creative productions is disappearing. That is sad because some of the greatest shows I've ever been in were done on the straw-hat circuit. It's impossible to believe what could be done in a week. There was something about the pressure that brought out the best in the actors. It was absolute insanity for ten weeks. Actors really went crazy, and the living together made for a strange wedding of people. Relationships were quickly made and broken, and no one behaved as he did at home.

My husband and I kept giving up our apartments and coming back and looking for new ones until we latched onto a cheap cold-water flat on West 50th Street between Ninth and Tenth avenues. It was one of my great finds even though it had a bathtub in the kitchen, a john in the hallway, and no heat, but the rent was only twenty-six dollars a month. It was then that I developed my intense hatred for Con Ed, which has lasted till this day, because, unlike the phone company which will allow calls to come in if you explain to them you are desperate, the gas people come to the door in the dead of winter and shut you off.

This was the most excruciating period of my life. I used to hear some actors say that they would give themselves five years to make it. That never entered my mind. I always felt that somehow it would happen. I don't know why. I think it's because I'm a natural optimist. I just can't understand how you could put a time limit on something you really want to achieve; either you're in it or you're not. I just felt that it would be all right and I refused to worry about it even though terrible things were happening to actors all around me.

My own relationship with Jim was fine. When either of us used to leave the house for a reading, I wondered what our thoughts would be when we came back up the four flights of stairs. What will have happened? Will it at last *be*? Often, I'd be waiting for him to climb those four flights after hearing the downstairs door open, hanging on to the sound of his footsteps. Once inside we'd take pleasure in dissecting every word that was said at the interview. We looked for friendly signs, and we celebrated if there was a call back. But everything we thought was going to lead somewhere always seemed to vanish. Now I realize that all the leads that paid off were gotten through people I knew in class. Nothing ever came from walking in cold.

My free-lancing for the phone company led to a steady job with the Screen Actors Guild. Unlike most other places which refused to hire actresses for permanent work, afraid that they would need time off, they understood my need for a flexible schedule and said I could stay as long as I liked. Calls would come in for film extras, and I would call my friends and tell them to rush over to casting, but that kind of work just didn't seem my style.

Fortunately, the guild took care of its workers. I was having a terrible problem with my teeth. Whenever a tooth hurt, I'd go to any dentist I'd find in the phone book.

Rather than have him fix it, I'd ask him to put me to sleep and pull the tooth. My whole mouth needed work because my teeth were crooked, but it was too expensive. I used to lie in bed and all my troubles would narrow down to something like "Oh, God, my teeth, why can't I fix them? My mouth is aching and I'm in agony." Everybody would say, "Oh, no, you've got to eat; you can't bother with your teeth." I applied to the guild for help, and in four days I received an appropriation of three hundred dollars to take care of the dentistry. All without humiliation.

I would have died if somebody had told me when I came to New York that it would take ten years for my career to get moving. My mother was no problem to me; she never expected me to marry a lawyer or a doctor. I looked forward to paying her visits because I knew I was going to be fed. She found me clothes and sent me money. When she came to New York, she'd go to one of the elegant hotels, and I'd stay with her for a week or so to remind myself what gracious living was like. In our house money had never been thought of as a great objective. My mother was a very independent woman.

For Americans, particularly male, money represents virility. It's their potency. If they don't have it, they slide down the other side. Actors and actresses who starved when they were young seem to be more destroyed by not getting ahead. I myself didn't have children, but there were many talents that were married, and once they had offspring, their problems were compounded. Women who stood by their actor husbands would turn on them once a child came and made the man feel guilty with accusations of failing as a provider. I began to notice that careers that were just beginning were falling off. Some really gifted people just disappeared. Even today I get letters from some of them. Wonderful actresses made the choice to be married to the man at home and remain there because, I guess, they felt degraded by what they had to go through. For me, there was no choice.

What we went through did affect my relationship with my husband. We were young when we got married in the typical correct way, at the Little Church Around the Corner. His background, however, was entirely different from mine. He had grown up in a family that wasn't well-to-do, and he had tremendous problems about not earning any money. He was extremely good-looking at a time when handsomeness was not considered likely to go hand-in-hand with talent, which was not true in his case. What we were was really good friends who had a need for each other. Even though he had a wonderful sense of humor and great understanding, we were destined to break up after thirteen years because we finally didn't have a marriage anymore. We had two people just surviving—and I'm the kind of person that's going to survive no matter what. That realization is what kept me going on. People say that I have tremendous strength, but to me it is intuitive and requires no effort. It was just something to endure. It never entered my mind to do anything else. I had no feeling about what was happening. My discouragements were not long-lasting. I had grown up in a family in which the woman was respected intellectually so I was primed to face my problems. Whatever difficulties I had to go through probably helped me and are worthwhile remembering. Now that that period of my life is over, I feel I wouldn't have had it any other way.

The theater has always meant freedom to me, and freedom has always been my aim. Remember, I once wanted to fly, to be free of everything and everybody. Somehow I get that feeling when I act on a stage. I can be complete and also somebody else. Once up there, I get rid of all those things—good, bad, or indifferent—I may feel about myself, and at the end of an evening I can be as charming and loving and whatever I need to be toward whomever I need to be with. Having just been something that represented being free, I become free—of my own free will!

Another satisfaction I get from my work is the realization that I am creating something that is completely mine. Now that I'm married again and have children, I find acting an even greater release. That business about being a wife and mother not being compatible with being an actress is a lot of nonsense. Acting gives me the opportunity of being a complete individual. When I enter a company, I come in only as myself. They are not interested in your children or your husband or anything personal. They just want to know what you can give them. You are taken care of, and you are treated with respect. When you go home, you are something else. Your family has the right to make that demand of you. That's the position you have taken with them. Some mornings you come down kicking the dogs, cats, and kids aside, and you say, "Okay, I've played this part long enough. I'm ready now to be addressed by someone as Miss Dewhurst. Do I want a cup of tea? Do I feel all right? Am I getting tired? Is there anything you can do for me to make me happy?"

Most of the time, though, you get in the car, ride back home, and open the door to a scream, "I have to be at football practice right away, Mother." Someone else says, "I'm not going to the store," and so forth. It's times like these, with my family, that seem so much more significant, having gone through the bad years. That period was not a waste, because if it had happened differently, I don't know what I would have been like. Were it to have come easily, I don't think I would have gone into the depths of myself as a person or as an actress. The crises I endured made me more determined that, once I had any degree of success, I would not let it go for nothing. Remembering that helps me with my discipline.

During a long run you lecture yourself this way: "So what if you don't want to go on tonight, remember the days you used to walk the street and say, 'My arm . . . my leg . . . you can have it, if only I could be up there.'"

I used to absorb all those rejections by some kind of osmosis, taking them in at the moment. I was lousy at making the rounds. Friends always came to my rescue. Once Hurd Hatfield, whom I worked with in summer stock, got me one of the weirdest acting jobs I've ever had. Some members of the old Polish aristocracy were having a gala night at the Waldorf-Astoria. I played Modjeska and from a box welcomed the guests with a Polish accent. The five dollars I was being paid was not the attraction, but the dinner that followed was. After I did my bit, I was escorted by a group of men to the buffet. Since they still addressed me as the character I portrayed, I felt I could not ruin their illusion by giving in to my hunger pangs. I pretended not to care about eating which was quite an acting feat in itself.

Some headway was made when I did a scene from *Desire Under the Elms* for Joe Anthony at the Theatre Wing. Even though I was young for the part, I wanted to do it very much, because I had always felt that O'Neill was my writer. I invited an agent, Jane Broder, whom I wanted to represent me very much. She told me that she liked what I had done and that I should lose weight, but there was no point in signing me because there was nothing she could do for me. Soon afterward, a production of the play was announced for the ANTA Theater. I called her to get me an interview. She pleaded for me, and finally they agreed to see me.

Harold Clurman, Robert Whitehead, and the stage manager were there for the reading, and it was painful. I happen to be a good reader, which has helped my career, and I could feel, when I was finished, Mr. Clurman was interested. Because he believes you can't really judge performers unless they do prepared scenes, he asked me to come back with something I'd worked on. My husband acted with me, and there was a great discussion afterward. Carol Stone was also being considered, and finally I got a call from the stage manager that she had gotten the part. The understudy had been hired before, and so they couldn't even offer me that, but they asked me to join the company that Mr. Clurman and Mr. Whitehead had formed.

While I was with them, they offered me a role in *Mrs. McThing* which I turned down because I preferred to do a small part in *Desire*. When I told my mother about my decision and that *Desire* closed on the night *McThing* opened, she said, "The name 'Helen Hayes' means nothing to you?"

At that time, Harold Clurman began his classes for actors which were at 11:30 P.M., so that those who were working could attend. Since I knew him, I was able to get in. He made observations that I will always remember. An important point was that he did not want to see us playing Hamlet or Lady MacBeth, using the day our dog died as our prop for sadness. Shakespeare's characters were great souls, and we would have to reach for them without relying on minor catastrophes. He also told us that it is a self-indulgence just to cry on stage, or to experience anything that may be true for us but not necessarily for the audience. He reminded us, by hitting the stage and saying, "You see this—this is a stage. You see that—that's not a door; it's a fake door. You have to bring the reality home, but you must do that in the character. Your personal experience cannot do it unless it can reach into what the person you are playing is going through."

He gave me scenes to prepare, and most of them were from classics. Reading Shakespeare, I thought, "What is this?" especially after all the realistic, earthbound, and kitcheny things I had been doing. Just as important as the tangible help he gave us in acting was the moral reinforcement. He told us what our lives should be like in order to be able to project ourselves on stage, and more than that, he helped us build our self-respect. We were reminded of the pride we should take in our profession. He knew that some of us didn't have the shoes to go for a job and that some of us couldn't pay the dry cleaners for the suit and that some of us had bad teeth and that all of these things became monstrous obstacles. Even so, the actor must fight for his profession. Although most of us listening didn't know where we were going or what we were doing, we felt more confident.

For the class I casually undertook Constance in *King John.* Since no one told me that you have to be incredible to do Shakespeare, I entered into it as I would any part. American actors can really surpass any from any country, including England, in doing Shakespeare because we're not too overloaded with tradition, and if your instrument is ready, you can come to it with greater passion.

From doing that part, I got a call from a man named Joseph Papp. He said that his wife was in my class and had told him of my performance. What he had in mind was to do scenes from Shakespeare in the basement of some small out-of-the-way church. Among the parts he wanted me to play was Juliet, and that stunned me so much that after I hung up, I thought that was the most peculiar phone call I had ever received. I didn't know then that it would also be the most important. It took another phone call from him to actually get me down to the church. Among the actors that were down there were J. D. Cannon and Roscoe Browne. We got to know and respect each other, and worked together as a dedicated group. I have an inclination to get involved, and when we put on our show, I realized I was really lucky to be working with Joseph Papp who is an absolute genius. What he had was a tremendous drive that made Shakespeare easy for us by helping us overcome the major difficulty we had: all the dialogue.

I wasn't paid anything for my work with Papp, but I was beginning to be a working actress and was able to sustain myself, not only from summer stock but also from the occasional theatrical jobs that would pop up. The Whitehead office was still interested in me, and when they were doing the late, great Tyrone Guthrie's production of *Tamburlaine,* I was among the many young girls who played virgins and concubines. English and Canadian actors had all the speaking parts. I tried out for a role of a virgin who had one pleading speech with the star, Anthony Quayle. Dr. Guthrie, reading people in his stocking feet, asked, "Dewhurst, who is Dew?" I was scared to death. During rehearsal the next day when we got to the part I'd tried out for, Dr. Guthrie said, "What's the matter? Are you going to read it, or are you just going to stand there?" I suppose my selling point was the fact that I was a Canadian and that the production would still be considered English-Canadian speaking. My disappointment came when I had to wear a veil throughout the show, and nobody knew who I was.

After our Toronto opening, the stars flew down for the New York run, and the supernumeraries had to take the train. At the station I was surprised to look up and see Dr. Guthrie and his wife coming across the waiting room. With his great hawk face and long, flowing, orange-knit scarf, he made a tremendous impression as he walked up and down the aisle of the train to talk with the minor members of the cast, concerned about what we were all doing. For me, this is the spirit of the theater.

During the limited run of the show, I just kept watching one woman's part, and it broke my heart that I wasn't playing it. When the show closed, Dr. Guthrie came to my dressing room and singled me out specifically to say that he enjoyed working with me and that he hoped it would happen again. I carried that for a month.

A year later I saw him at a theater and went up to him and said I had worked for him. He replied, "You're Colleen Dewhurst, and I remember you very well." Sometime later, I was doing *Macbeth* in Central Park. It rained, and the stage was so slippery that we could not even begin. Everybody ran, but there was a man in the fifth row with a newspaper over his head waiting for that performance. Dr. Guthrie would have us play and would have stayed there, no matter what. I felt that he had watched for me to make it and had come to see how I would do. Seeing him sit there like that was very moving.

In stock, I continued to play all kinds of parts, and many of them were in strange situations. I was Beauty in *Beauty and the Beast* with an actor who was about two inches shorter than myself and ten years younger. Every time I came through the forest, the audience collapsed with laughter. In *Mister Roberts*, I was ridiculous as the cute nurse when they dressed me up in a wig and a costume they flew in from New York that fit me like a mini outfit, and I had to say seductively, "Hi, fellas." My height and my vocal equipment were a little too much.

Edward Everett Horton loathed me when I first did *Springtime for Henry* with him. I was not his type at all. He liked his leading ladies to be chic. After doing all my rehearsals in slacks, I showed for dress rehearsal in a skirt; he commented, "Oh, Miss Dewhurst *has* legs!" There was a sort of armed truce between the two of us, and he would go around muttering, "Line first, business second." I looked at him as a stand-up comedian while I was an actress. There was a spot in the show where I stepped on his foot and I said something. After the opening, he told me, "In that bit, dear, line first, business second." Even though it bothered me, I did what he said the next night, and the laughter lasted a five full minutes. I looked at him with respect after that.

My association with Edward Everett Horton continued when he called me and my husband to do a three-character play with him on tour. The hundred dollars or so a week that we got paid was fabulous, but I still could not afford the elegant dress the character I was playing would wear. He told me to pick out a costume and made sure the manager paid me for it. At rehearsal he studied me, and then sent out for shoes to go with it. His sensitivity was overwhelming.

One night while we were in Pennsylvania with the show, I got a call at our motel from Joe Papp. He had just done *Julius Caesar* in an amphitheater on the Lower East Side, off the drive. "I want you to do Kate in *The Taming of the Shrew*," he said. "I can't pay you, and nobody comes scouting. We sent out for every agent, producer, and critic, but they didn't show up. It's up to you if you want to do it." I agreed immediately, but only if I could get a release from the show. I went to Edward, and he asked me, "Are you getting paid?" When I said no, he replied, "All right, do as you like."

Rehearsing out by the East River Drive was an unusual experience for an actress in New York, because there were trees and the river. We didn't even mind the 90-degree temperature. By a strange juxtaposition of fate, while preparing for this production, which was to become the real start of my career, my mother was in the hospital dying.

Without money we had to improvise everything from props to costumes. Everyone pitched in to make the production work. And it did! Opening night the place was mobbed with the most interesting audience I've ever played to. All of them were from the neighborhood, many of them Jewish immigrants from Russia and Poland who studied the play before they came. What appealed to them, too, I think, was that it was a perfect place to go and bring their children on a hot summer night to get away from their tenements. I had been warned that I would hear from these people, but when they first yelled out at me, as the audience used to in Shakespeare's day, it was a shock. I couldn't believe the way they screamed during one of the big fights between Kate and Petruchio, warning him, "Watch out!" "Look, here she comes!" "Oh, God, stop her!" One night, when we got to the part where Kate submits and falls to her knees while Petruchio delivers his soliloquy about the way to tame a woman, a man way in the back shouted, "Aw, give her a pillow." It was such heaven, because you knew that you had succeeded in the play coming full turn to where they were saying, "Okay, she's had enough now. She's paid."

During a daytime performance, one 98-degree day, under a sun that was blinding me during the wooing scene, I felt faint. Now, I'm not a girl who ever faints. There I was standing up there to give a speech on men and love. Suddenly, I heard the audience begin to laugh, and I looked down to see a little boy who had wandered to the edge of the stage, standing and staring with only a T-shirt on and his bottom showing. He was fascinated, and so I reached out and took his hand. We both turned and faced the house while I continued my soliloquy on what men are. Everyone roared.

The people in the neighborhood used to follow us around to talk to us. They loved our scenery and props. The swords were of particular interest to them. It seemed to relate to their environment. I used to think it was their way of getting rid of the kind of aggressive energy which our male actors used in a more creative way.

Everyone called various agents, and nobody came. Still hoping to be handled by Jane Broder, I phoned her, and down she came with her sister. Her enthusiasm was encouraging. Word must have gotten out about us, because several nights later Arthur Gelb, a critic from *The New York*

Times, showed up. Unfortunately, after the wooing scene, it started to pour. When the performance was called off, he came backstage to meet Joe Papp, who later told me Gelb was all agog and wondered who we were, where did we come from, and how did we wind up down there?

The next day, Mr. Gelb came out with a most positive critique. Seeing your first review in *The New York Times* is a very exciting moment for any actress. Mr. Gelb made us sound so appealing that our audience was suddenly displaced by the suit-and-tie crowd of the Upper East Side. Gone was the *joie* of our old followers, and we really had to work hard not to be intimidated by their replacements. I really knew we were a success when agents began to call me, but I still remembered how Miss Broder endured our concrete seats before they were cushioned by the *Times* review. That's why I called her to tell her I had two or three offers to sign with other agents but that I preferred to go with her. We've had a great association ever since.

Now, I thought, I was on my way, especially because I was then offered the role of Camille in a real Off-Broadway production at the Cherry Lane Theatre. Every actress wants to do great parts like that, but I should have known better. My performance of a woman dying of consumption was overshadowed by my 145 pounds of deeply tanned flesh. I pleaded with the girl doing costumes to put sleeves on the gowns, but she wouldn't listen and I came out looking like I could beat my way out of the place. I had no sense of humor about the reviews, though. They killed us. Walter Kerr, referring to what we thought was our abandon, said, "Last night at the Cherry Lane they laughed and laughed and laughed." Brooks Atkinson noted that he could not believe, when I went coughing into my death, that I would not rise in my full white gown and take my curtain call. Jerry Tallmer was the most disparaging of all when he wrote, "Marguerite is a white, fluttering moth. Miss Dewhurst is a full-blooded luna."

Going through the awful second night of that flop was an education in the strength an actress needs. Though there was absolute silence backstage, I had to put cotton batting in my ears to deaden the noise that was coming from the audience. We were set to play out the week, and to fill the house, tickets were sent to the USO. From the time those soldiers and sailors spotted our elegant gentlemen bowing and prancing around they howled. One scene, however, always captured everyone, and that is the confrontation between Armand's father and me. Joe Barr, who played the old man, really got them, and it shows that no matter what the production is like, if an actor really does it, the audience can be his.

From that tragedy I went into another, *The Eagle Has Two Heads*. Who could resist playing such a grande dame? Tallmer hit it on the head a second time in referring to my death scenes by starting off with "Colleen Dewhurst dies again," and wound up with "Will someone please give this girl a job so she can stop doing these things!"

That "someone" turned out to be José Quintero. It seemed that I was appearing everywhere that season, and I was regarded as the queen of Off Broadway, even winning some award. That was the time I also did Lady Macbeth for the Shakespeare festival. We had moved up to Central Park and now had quite a bit of prestige. I must admit I was just all right in the part but not good enough. Sometimes a lot of people think you're perfect for a role, and you do, too, but something goes wrong in the chemistry of the production that can affect the actor, and the results are disappointing, not only to the people who are rooting for you but also, most of all, to the performer. I hope I have a chance to redeem myself as Lady Macbeth in the future. In spite of all these less than spectacular exposures, José must have been impressed by something I had done because he offered me the lead, without even reading for it, in *Children of Darkness*.

In the third act of the play, there was a wonderful gentleman who showed up, Lord Wainwright. A week before the opening the actor who played the part dropped out, and José was anxious for a replacement. He wanted to know if we had any suggestions, and I brought up the name of one actor, while J. D. Cannon recommended George C. Scott.

I had been taken to see George's work only a short while before by J.D.'s wife, who thought he would be the perfect Antony to my Cleopatra in the projected Papp production at the Heckscher Theater. At that time he was in the Shakespeare Festival's production of *Richard III*, and when I saw him on the stage in this show, I was immediately antagonistic even though I knew he was great! I think the reason for my attitude was that I resented his having been brought in by Papp from nowhere, while my husband, who was having so much trouble, had not been considered. So, I turned to Alice and said, "He's too short!" I knew that was untrue, but I couldn't help myself. All Alice could do was exclaim, "What!"

When J.D. brought up George's name, all I said was "I think the actor I want for the part is perfect." José being impetuous, replied, "We're going to call these two actors, and whoever is home is going to be hired on the spot." The one I was rooting for was called first and, as chance would have it, was out, but George was in.

As soon as George arrived, J.D. introduced us, and I was still vaguely harsh. Since George had to step into the part quickly, José, who usually never walks through a part for an actor, showed him what he wanted. George just sat there and watched beneath his heavy lids. José asked, "Shall I do it again?" George replied, "No, thank you," and got up to walk it in his arresting way.

On opening night, Jane Broder said to me, "Darling, you were absolutely splendid, but that man, what's-his-name, just comes in and ties it up and takes it home." That made me furious, especially when he got all the reviews. J.D. and I worked like hell for two acts, and in he came in the last one and took over the show. I realized he was not as short as I had thought, but I was still determined to see him that way. During the run, George and I were very formal with each other; I was Miss Dewhurst, and he was Mr. Scott to me, always.

George was very much of a loner, so we didn't get to know each other until one night when I had forgotten the keys to my apartment. My husband was always home except that one time. I went into Jack Delaney's bar to try to phone him, and there was no answer. I was stunned, and on coming out of the phone booth, I noticed George sitting by himself at the bar. Since I was upset, and he was the only one I knew there, I went up to him and said, "Would you mind, Mr. Scott, if I sat with you for a little while?" He agreed, and I went on to explain what had happened. We moved to a table, and we sat and talked. This was the first time we had made any real contact. I kept interrupting our conversation to try my apartment, but I'd get no answer. We were there until the bar closed at four in the morning, talking and really getting to know each other. He walked me to my place. I went up and tried the door and came back down. I asked him to take me to the Cannons' where I thought I might spend the night. They were very gracious about it, but when they saw George with me, they were surprised. I believe that, after I left the next day, my friends turned to each other with an "Uh-huh!"

José was asked to do a drama for the Spoleto festival. He chose O'Neill's *A Moon for the Misbegotten* and put me in the lead. By the time I was ready to leave that summer, George and I had realized that we were in love and were determined to share our lives. Since both of us were married, it was like murdering everyone around us, but we had no choice.

Working with José, a volatile Panamanian, on a script

Colleen Dewhurst and George C. Scott in performance of

about repressed New Englanders taught me a great deal. He evoked a kind of spontaneity and released our passions and drives. Often, you would find yourself crying when most people would expect you to be laughing—and vice versa. This original way of thinking, I believe, is unique in our time.

Antony and Cleopatra (Photograph by George E. Joseph)

Today everybody tries to categorize things. This is a time of books that teach us everything, from how to face the day and live to how to go to bed and love. Relationships lack immediacy because everybody is studying everybody else. As soon as people meet you, they want to know your Zodiac sign, what your hang-ups are, and whether you've been in analysis. With these embarrassing beginnings, it's no wonder we never get to know each other's natural self.

On my return, George and I did that *Anthony and Cleopatra* together, after all. Now we were one, except when we entered the theater. He knew we had to split up when working with others, because everybody gets kind of nervous thinking you've formed a clique. We intentionally stayed apart and tried to avoid talking about our work when we were alone. Everything George knew about the theater came intuitively because he never studied acting. When he came out of the marines, he went back to college to major in journalism at the University of Missouri. A part in one of their productions convinced him to become an actor.

José was doing the National Educational Television production of *Medea* with Dame Judith Anderson, and cast me, along with Jacqueline Brookes and Betty Miller, in the chorus. Miss Anderson is very short, but she didn't flinch at my five-foot-eight height towering over her. As I studied her with fascination, I grew to love her because I felt that she appreciated being surrounded by people with talent—a rare thing in the theater. Too often an actress will think she will shine brighter if there are lesser lights around her. This is a self-deception, because unless everybody is great onstage, you will never reach beyond yourself. The better the rest of the cast, the better you are.

Cueing other actors onstage is something I don't approve of. One night, however, we were in rehearsal for *Medea* when Dame Judith went up on her lines, and the stage manager was not on the ball, so we were all standing and waiting. The moment grew longer and longer, until finally I threw the cue, and she continued. At the conclusion of the scenes Dame Judith said, as she passed me, "Ready to play the part, are you?" We all broke up. It seemed as if she was saying she was glad that we were good.

There is nothing one actress can learn from another. I hardly ever go to plays except to see friends perform. It's disaster to try to copy or try to adjust to other people's ideas. Whatever you have to offer in the theater, as an individual, is going to come across to those who want to receive what you have to give. You cannot be everybody's cup of tea. That's a difficult lesson to learn, but that's what it's all about. Sometimes, if I see an actor perform, I feel I just don't want to meet him in person or have anything to do with him. A psychoanalyst with an actor for a patient could learn so much about him if he could watch him in rehearsal periods. It's strange what an actor chooses to play before a director.

At first reading I may look at an actor and say to myself, "Now, there's a really attractive man." Then he begins to interpret and I'll think, "No, no, no!" He may choose to whine his way through a love scene, play violence with tears in his eyes, or portray rage highly strident, and I say to myself, "Hm, I can see where that's going." Then, somebody else whom you haven't noticed at all will get up to do a scene with you, and you'll say, "Wow!" because total contact with this person has been made from the beginning. He is able to look at you and work with you immediately without the preliminaries of saying anything directly to you. You just seem to move together, and you know that something is happening.

George felt the same way I did about Dame Judith, having just completed a short run with her in the Broadway production of *Comes a Day*. Again, he walked off with the play, but she didn't try to cut him out. On the contrary, she insisted on giving him his curtain call.

My big TV break came when the Producers of the NET series did *Don Quixote* with Lee J. Cobb and Eli Wallach, and they asked me to stand by for Dulcinea. Finally, they decided to let me do the part. Those were the days of live

TV that kept all the adrenalins perking. When the little red light on the camera flashed, you got the feeling you were onstage. My confidence was greater with my teeth fixed.

Now, George and I began moving into the money area. He went out to Hollywood to do *Anatomy of a Murder*, and when he came back, he went into *The Andersonville Trial*. At the same time I became a star on Broadway for the first time, in *Caligula*. Being up there seemed much less important than my emotional involvement with George and the fact that I was pregnant. Right after having the baby, I went into another Broadway show, *All the Way Home*. Because George kept coming when we were trying out in Boston, the producer warned me, "Whatever you do, don't get pregnant." I lied, and said, "No, sir," knowing I already was. The show had a long run, because it won the Pulitzer Prize, and finally I had to give an Act of God notice. Luckily I was playing a pregnant woman, and they allowed me to continue. All they had to do was change the line "You don't show much" to "You show, Mary." To be able to play up until a few weeks before the baby was born was ideal. On matinee days, I could almost hear the women in the audience speculating, "Is that some kind of padding?" until they couldn't help but realize it was all me.

I suppose George and I could have played it safe and held out for bigger and better movie and television offers, but somehow the gravy didn't mean anything unless we had the meat of real theater, and that didn't mean Broadway success, either. After making a big splash in the movie *The Hustler*, George decided to go in with Ted Mann and José to form the Theater of Michigan Company in his hometown of Detroit. This was supposed to be the first of many such repertoire groups all over the country. One thing I learned from that experience was that, if it wasn't for the Jewish people, the theater would be dead. To raise backing for our two initial productions, Ira Levin's *General Seeger* and Alice

Cannon's *Great Day in the Morning*, we solicited funds
through the mails until we were stopped by the authorities.
There we were stuck in an expensive hotel while our money
was running out. In order to arouse interest, we performed
scenes in the homes of the so-called elite of Detroit. They
turned out to be the local La Dolce Vita crowd. It was not
until we were booked into the Jewish homes that we were
treated with respect. Ready for us, they listened without a
drink in their hands. They understood what we were there
for and showed their approval by writing checks.
Unfortunately, however, there were not enough of them.

A final attempt was made by throwing a huge party which
we charged to our hotel bill. So few people showed up that
we knew we had lost. Depressed, we went to bed when Ted,
who had been ready to give up on the idea long before,
suddenly appeared, asking where the fund-raising brochures
were because he felt impelled to distribute them. His
hysteria overwhelmed us. Then next morning the one thing
we knew was that we had to get out without facing the
hotel management. We put on all the clothes we had, even
overdressing the two children, and made our escape.

That was seven or eight months out of our lives. We got
Seeger on in New York, and it played two nights. Though
Great Day only played ten performances, I think years from
now people will realize what a great play it is. When it
closed, Harold Clurman came to George and said, "You've
got to learn one thing as a producer, George: no more of
your own money." To realize his Theater of Michigan
dream, George had sold himself to a television series and to
a two-year movie contract, and sunk the money into the
project. Now it was all gone, and rather than to declare
bankruptcy, we went out to Hollywood to work at anything
to pay off every penny we owed.

Desire Under the Elms brought us back to Off Broadway.
We were so excited about the parts that, even after we'd get

into bed at night, George would jump up with an inspiration on how to make a scene work. Then we'd try it out in the bedroom, but he would never be satisfied with an idea until he got the response he wanted before an audience. Unless the people out there buy it, no concept is worth a damn. Greater consciousness of the house is what I've gotten from working with George.

Working Off Broadway you realize that no matter how much good wine and champagne you drink, you just wind up with a wonderful headache and that just plain water can be so much more refreshing. You've got to go back there to refire your inspiration and to find out what the theater is all about. Off Broadway everybody's doing what they can for the love of it. You come to Broadway with high hopes that go down the drain with the money spent on sets and costumes. Uptown everyone is so intense about being a success that whether you're good, bad, or indifferent really doesn't matter. Though I came off well with the critics for my Broadway shows, *The Ballad of the Sad Café* and *More Stately Mansions*, neither of them was a smash.

As far as movies are concerned, my appearances in *The Nun's Story* and *A Fine Madness* did not require what I call acting. I admit I did it for the money. I was in particular financial difficulty when George got the seven-year-itch and left me for Ava Gardner. We were divorced for two years, but we got back together again and remarried.

The theater today is looked upon as a director's theater, but there are so few Josés, Kazans, Penns, and Papps around. Too many can't assume the absolute power required of a director. He must have the ability to knit the company together, so that it will fight to the death for the production. Unless the actors go out there as a unit, they become intimidated. An actor must perform with authority. He can't be soft. It takes a very hearty soul to keep going.

Half the time he's not supported by the director. This is the man who must have tremendous courage. He must be able to deal with his actors, writers, and stage manager with a strong hand yet show that he has understanding and complete respect. The control must come from the top. You feel that he is stepping out there with you. He makes you believe that this is the way he wanted it, and this is the way it is. Too often an actor likes a director because he doesn't bother him. Most of the time you're dealing with a personality that has no point of view whatsoever or is hoping that you and the other actors will take over because he doesn't know how to, and if he's not too destructive and let's you work, you may come out all right. The better ones I've worked with can give it back to the actor by watching you do something in a scene which may be way off from what it should be, yet encourage you to keep going so that you might come up with the right answer. He may say, as José often does, "I do question what you're doing, so I think we should try another approach." Never "That's wrong." The most important contribution of a director is that you feel you have a potential for a height and that he keeps you working till you find out what it is. God help you if you ever reach it. You hope you will never find it. Safety calls for a certain topper to be put on you that you choose. Unless you have someone behind you who can give you the confidence to go further and demand more of the best of you, you cannot make it in the theater—just as in life.

I know I have a reputation of being an actor's actor. That comes from being able to afford to work wherever my integrity takes me. I keep coming back to Off Broadway as someone does to his roots. It's like the story about the man who is in Europe and says to you, "The American must stay over here. Your artistry will be recognized. The United States is a seething pit." To that you feel like replying,

"Baby, it's up to you to return and do something. Don't sit over here in the cafés and ignore what's going on. You can lose your talent that way."

You enter those bleak Off-Broadway houses and go to the dressing room to hang up your coat; then suddenly you feel you are home. Everyone understands each other, and you know why you are there. All those black, misty-looking theaters look like wombs when you come in. Somehow something seems to work down there that doesn't happen uptown.

You can't think of acting as a profession that you're going to take anything from. You can't use it—it's just not usable. You can't give it a certain amount of time. After ten years I felt, "I'm ready for gracious living. I want a private bathroom, and gorgeous gowns." The basic thing is that it has to be given you professionally, otherwise what do these things matter?

VIII
The Composer:
JERRY HERMAN
Parade to Broadway

I NEVER thought song writing, which was my hobby, would become my career. Then one day, through a friend of a friend, I obtained an appointment with a song publisher who actually bought the first song I had ever written. I realized at that moment that this was something I might be able to do for a living.

The only theatrical experience I'd had until that time was as dramatics counselor at my father's summer camp for children. That place was quite an operation, a really professional plant. During the summer only the children were involved in the productions, but at the end of the season the adults connected with the camp played in one big show. Producing such musicals as *Paint Your Wagon* and *A Tree Grows in Brooklyn* gave me the ideal background as to how shows are put together. It was almost a summer-stock theater by the time I left—what Tamiment or Green Mansions had been to other writers.

Then before going to college, I wrote a musical especially for Phyllis Newman, a friend from Jersey City—a charity benefit for the Jewish Community Center. This and selling my first song encouraged me to concentrate on furthering my musical-theater education.

I had heard that the University of Miami had an experimental drama department where students wrote, performed, did the sets for and costumed their own productions. It was important to me to get a basic college education at a school where I would be able to write and to see some of my things done.

Feeling my way along at the university, I started slowly by writing a few songs for a production, then directed a show, costumed one, and finally wrote the music and lyrics for a small, original work, *An Apple for Venus*, which won a trophy and caused quite a stir. The plot, based on the legend of Helen of Troy, was told in a light, spoofing manner—similar to *The Golden Apple* which appeared two or three years later. When *Apple* came on, I felt pleased because I realized that, although I was just a young kid, I had thought of using the same material established writers had chosen. All this convinced me I was right in seriously pursuing a career as a composer-lyricist.

My most spectacular production at college was a ninety-man varsity show at Dade County Auditorium which had enormous sets and a revolving stage. The school invested in it heavily, but it paid off quite well.

What I got out of my shows at the University of Miami and at my father's camp was that I was able to see what worked and what didn't by actually experimenting before an audience. I found out that you can't really be taught theater in a classroom—you can't theorize. If you make a mistake onstage, you get an immediate reaction and know what *not* to do again. It's the only way to develop. All those years I was learning by doing.

This prepared me for *I Feel Wonderful*, a revue for the Studio M Little Theatre in Miami. I was offered the opportunity to do this as a result of my college successes. George Keathley, who directed the 1965 Broadway revival of *The Glass Menagerie*, was then director of this group. He asked me if I would be interested in doing a musical there because he wanted to diversify his repertoire. I saw this as a great opportunity for me to do professional, out-of-school theater immediately after graduating, and so I stayed down there for about six months, working on all phases of the show. The reception was so enthusiastic that my father and several Miami businessmen decided to bring it to New York.

The whole thing was done swiftly Off Broadway and closed just as quickly—but it gave me my start. I was playing piano in the show's small orchestra, and after a performance an attractive woman came over to me. She said, "I'm Priscilla Morgan of the William Morris Agency, and I'd like to have lunch with you tomorrow." I felt on top of the world when they signed me soon after. Finding an agent of that caliber made the whole *I Feel Wonderful* experience worthwhile.

Again, it was doing, being seen, and having my work heard that was the answer. This is the major contribution that Off Broadway can make. You can write the most brilliant things . . . you can have your briefcase filled with gems . . . yet they mean nothing unless they're played before an audience, and people can hear them in their proper place—in the theater.

When I had come to Manhattan, I had rented a walk-up in Greenwich Village—a one-room affair typical of what you would expect a starving composer to have. I was more fortunate than most because I had some furniture that I was able to take from home, making it much more pleasant than the empty garret usually is. Of course, there was a piano, and I did a great deal of writing.

I had another bonus in that I was able to earn a living by playing the piano. I immediately got jobs in nightclubs, which left my days free for writing and for making rounds. Just a few hours' work at night allowed me to function at my craft all day.

All the while, William Morris set up auditions and showed me to everybody in New York, but that didn't work. I can understand the rejections. After all, I was a young kid, and who would trust me locked in a hotel room in Philadelphia with a half-million-dollar production riding on my youthful talent? That's actually what one producer said to me. During this time, all that happened was that I sold some special material to the Garry Moore television show and to the Ray Bolger *Washington Square* program.

I realized that my work needed greater exposure. I was determined to get another show on, using all the material I had been writing that year, even if I had to present it in the streets.

Then, through some friends, I heard about a little nightclub in the Village, the Showplace. One afternoon I walked in there with my briefcase and said to Mr. Eilers, "I have some stuff here that I'd like you to hear." Even he, Off Broadway, on West Fourth Street, was very skeptical about me because of my youth. He put me off by saying, "Next week some time, when I have some time." I kept after him, and the following week I made an appointment. I played the material that was to become the show *Nightcap*—he was immediately sold. We set out together as producers, putting on the show that I look upon as the actual beginning of my career.

We held open auditions and found four people who were exceptionally talented: Charles Nelson Reilly, who later played a lead in *Hello, Dolly!* Kenneth Nelson, who went on to star in *The Fantasticks*, Fia Karen, a marvelous singer who afterward became the toast of Paris, and Jane Romano who just before she died was Ethel Merman's stand-by in *Gypsy*. With just me at the piano, the four of us really created history down there—this was pre-Julius Monk, and before the Off-Broadway revue was "in." It was the first show of its kind to amount to anything and played four hundred performances—unheard of for Off Broadway at that time.

I adapted *Nightcap*, which was originally conceived for the theater, into a cabaret show in two acts for a room full of tables and chairs where drinks were served. The material was made up mostly of spoofs of then current political situations. We satirized Rockefeller campaigning for governor and called it "Just Plain Folks." The performers impersonating the Rockefellers were dressed in mink and top hat, and accompanied themselves on guitars as they tried to convince the public that they were just one of the people. Then there was a satirical number on the first sack dress and another on the kidnapping of a movie star for publicity purposes. Whatever people were talking about we made fun of. We kept changing the show to keep it fresh. What really made it different from the usual cabaret show is that interspersed with the comedy were some beautifully sung ballads. This balance between the zany and the lovely made *Nightcap* special.

Before I started earning money on this show, there was a rehearsal in my apartment that turned out to be a catastrophe. In his effusion, Charles Nelson Reilly kicked over a table with my only dishes on it, and for weeks I had absolutely nothing to eat on—that was the kind of budget I had. There wasn't an extra dollar in those days, and when the cups and saucers were broken, they couldn't be replaced until we opened and were a hit.

It turned out that we were a greater success than I had dreamed possible. The critics came down and wrote enthusiastic comments, likening me to Rodgers and Hart. Danton Walker was particularly kind to me and mentioned the show column after column.

One Saturday night, after we had been playing three months, I walked over from my little apartment for the performance, and there was a line that went clear around the corner. That's when I realized that what had started out to be just a little showcase for the five of us had become an enormous smash.

It was a marvelous two years for me. I was earning money each week doing what I loved full time. Besides playing the piano nightly and adding new material, I was busy with all the facets of the production: seeing to the repair of sets and costumes, helping with publicity, being interviewed to promote the show, and taking care of business records. Because of the long run we replaced the cast and myself twice—which meant, of course, there were auditions and rehearsals for me to conduct.

Nightcap started a chain reaction. After a performance, a man named Larry Kasha came up to me and said, "I'd like to do your show in a theater," and *Parade* was born.

For name value, we got Dody Goodman who at that time was very big on Jack Paar's *Tonight* television show. Charles and Fia were kept, and a dancer was added. The show was expanded only slightly, since we wanted to keep it an intimate production. This time we had a four-piece band with me at the piano. We got Gary Smith, who has since become a well-known television designer, to do the sets which were more elaborate than the ones we had before.

The cost of putting on *Parade* at the Players Theatre was about twenty thousand dollars. Larry Kasha raised most of the money through his contacts and through backers' auditions for which I played.

Although I directed *Parade*, I decided to start specializing in what I felt I did best—composing and lyric writing. All the other phases of production that I had done previously, I realized, were only a means to present my music and lyrics to their best advantage.

Unlike *Nightcap*, *Parade* was not an enormous success, but it brought the critics down to see my work and gave me my first show album. It caught the attention of people who would not ordinarily have known about me.

Once again Off Broadway was to serve a great function in my career. Three months after *Parade* had opened and business had fallen off seriously, making it apparent that the show wasn't going to last much longer, and I was most discouraged, Gerald Ostreicher, a real-estate man who had dabbled in the theater by investing and coproducing, approached me to do what was to become my first Broadway musical, *Milk and Honey*.

Don Appell, a playwright who was also handled by William Morris, had an idea for a musical set in Israel. Both he and Mr. Ostreicher were told about me by Priscilla Morgan and were advised to see my show so that they could sample my work.

The two of them went down to see *Parade*, liked what they saw, and decided that they wanted me to be the composer-lyricist for their musical. At first, I questioned the whole thing and thought it was too fantastic to be true. Realization that the offer was concrete came at a lunch with Mr. Ostreicher, at which he presented me with a check to be used for a trip to

Israel to research its native music. The rest happened so fast that before I knew it I was on a plane with Don Appell to write a musical about which I hadn't even the remotest idea a few weeks before.

All this came from a show that wasn't a financial success Off Broadway! Without *Parade* I would never have gotten *Milk and Honey*, and without *Milk and Honey*, David Merrick would not have come to an Actor's Fund Benefit and offered me the chance to do *Hello, Dolly!* One show led to another, and it all stemmed from Off Broadway!

Once I hit Broadway and was well received, I returned to Off Broadway to do a labor of love, *Madame Aphrodite.* This show was based on a play by Tad Mosel, another client of Priscilla Morgan's. I had seen it on television four years before, and when I met Tad, I told him I thought it would make a most unusual musical.

Later, everyone told us it was *too* unusual. Among the experimental techniques that we used was an offstage chorus singing people's thoughts which gave emotional punch to a situation the way an orchestra usually does. My theory was, and still is, that we suspend disbelief, as far as the orchestra is concerned; we are schooled to accept the sound of those musicians and all those fiddles even in an intimate situation. We don't consider this an intrusion. We accept it totally. Why can't we be trained to accept twenty-five voices coming into the same room if there is an emotional reason for their presence? So effective and successful was this concept to me that I hope to use it again.

The central character herself was quite offbeat, a fascinating woman who sold fraudulent beauty products because her own physical ugliness made her despise beauty. She was bitter and hard, yet touching at the same time—very different from Dolly Levi and Auntie Mame in that they have a love of life. The musical essence of Madame Aphrodite's character was just as exciting to me as theirs. There is no formula or way of explaining why I choose material to musicalize. It is just my instinct.

Everything I've ever written comes from a character having to express a particular sentiment at a particular moment in a show. I've never written individual songs for the pop market. Frankly, I don't even know how to. I only write scores. The fact that my songs have caught on delights me, but they were only written as part of a musical framework.

The plot of *Madame Aphrodite* concerned itself with the love affair between a young salesman the harridan had hired and a plain girl that he meets and becomes interested in. As the girl uses one of the phony beauty creams, he believes she is becoming prettier when, in reality, it is love that is endowing her with beauty in his eyes.

The reason I did *Madame Aphrodite* Off Broadway was that I felt it belonged in a very intimate theater. I was also afraid it would have been commercialized and lost in one of the Broadway houses.

When I saw the actual production at the Orpheum Theatre, I realized that this wasn't the show I wanted it to be. As a Broadway production it might have been, that's the ironic thing about it. As it was, it failed not only for the critics and the public but also for myself. It ran for two weeks.

How strange it felt to have a hit on Broadway and a flop Off Broadway at the same time!

The major thing I learned from this catastrophe was I could overcome the setback by starting a new project. The day after the reviews I went to the piano and wrote a melody I had no idea what to do with. It wasn't for anything specific, but the morning after the disaster, I looked in the mirror and had a talk with myself, stirring up my creative juices again. I learned to face utter failure, which up to that point I had never experienced. Once more Off Broadway taught me something very valuable—a show might close the Saturday night after the opening, and I'll have to look in that mirror again. Because of what happened with *Madame Aphrodite,* I know that I can handle the situation.

After that debacle, I was able to go on to write *Hello, Dolly!*

When I think of the Off-Broadway days, I remember the excitement, which I no longer have, of being part of a show. I loved going to the theater every night and actually being in the production, and the feeling of rapport that all of us had in *Nightcap*. There was a wonderful spirit that I wouldn't want to trade for any of the glamour in my career now.

I miss the madcap rehearsals that were straight out of a Judy Garland-Mickey Rooney musical. There I was hanging red velour drapes and at the same time shouting various instructions to somebody else while Fia would be off in a corner singing. Neither of us were disturbed by Charles Nelson Reilly doing a monologue and clowning around, nor by a dog running wild and barking because his master, who was busy sewing the costumes, couldn't walk him. It was a scene from *Babes in Arms*.

Off Broadway was all fun—even the work and the difficulties. It is unfortunate that the nature of Broadway doesn't have this combustion.

I'm grateful for everything that happened in those days and that I am one of the people who have had the chance to be enriched by the Off-Broadway experience.

(Photograph by Charmian Reading)

IX

The Naked Stage:
LENNOX RAPHAEL and CHE!

The Symbolism of Sex

CHE GUEVARA was captured, had his battle wounds washed down, his body made beautiful, and was brought before the President of the United States who wanted to make love to him but had him killed instead, because Che refused to change ideological bed partners and showed his defiance by biting the President's penis. This dream I had became the play *Che!* for which we nine people involved in the production were charged by the city of New York with fifty-four counts such as public lewdness, consensual sodomy, and conspiracy to violate public morality, and were faced with spending most of our lives in prison.

My basic theme for everything I've written since 1966 is that sexual repression fosters political repression. In some mysterious way, this idea came to me after having been unable to write for three weeks because of the trauma of being nearly killed in an automobile accident in Morocco. I then wrote a long article on sex and politics, considering the appeal of Kennedy over Nixon, and observed that because we are obsessed with television, which often gets into bed with us, the public responded to the one with the most physicality.

I went on to do a play on Malcom X which almost was produced in Paris. Still juiced up by a new awareness, I returned to New York. When I couldn't get anybody really interested in my work, I did nothing for a year until I wrote *The Big Bad Fuck,* a long poem in which the leaders of the world got together to come together. Receiving no encouragement, I began to find it less and less important what people thought of me or of what I wrote. I realized that a writer has to forget about society's values and divorce his ego from his environment so that he can become closer to his true function, that of being a messenger who transmits his dream to paper.

Che! was part three of the sex-and-politics exploration, and at that point it no longer mattered to me whether I was a writer or whether I made it. I just had to do what was on my mind. I had always felt that life is the supreme fantasy in which the only environment that really exists is in your own head, and it was becoming that way for me. My thoughts were dominated by the fact that people so easily accept being slaves who keep masters—as I witnessed in my early life in Latin America—and that they receive so much sensual solace from killing—as in Vietnam—and so the play came into being. Ché Guevara was the total expression of my own beliefs, because he was a man who tried to make the world into what he thought it should be.

A couple of people were immediately interested in putting on the play, but they changed their minds. A year later I decided to produce *Che!* with Ed Wode, the writer and director of *Christmas Turkey,* one of the first plays in New York City to use nudity in characterization. We went into rehearsal at the Free Store Theatre in the East Village for two months, starting in February of '68, and worked ten hours a day with actors who answered our advertisements in *Show Business* and *Backstage*.

The plot is almost completely a seduction scene that takes place in the President's quarters. In addition to Che and the President, the other characters are the Sister of Mercy, Che's defender, a composite of the nun who was actually at the assassination of Ché and Tanya, an intimate of Ché's suspected of being a double agent for the Russians and the Cubans; Mayfang, a bisexual Secret Service freak; Breakstone Fearless, a Hollywood movie director; and Chili Billy, the son of King Kong, who was written in for my friends who dig him and who also represents the Second Coming of Christ.

There is constant sexual interplay between all the characters to dramatize the power struggle between America and Cuba. When Che goes down on the President or vice versa, it is an expression of political aggression and oppression. Sister of Mercy may screw with Che, but only because she needs his semen as evidence in his defense. Even her screams of delight when the son of Kong is on top of her represent the submission to our baser instincts by even the most fanatic puritans of ecstacy. The President takes a crap and wipes his ass onstage to show his attitude toward the people. All these may titillate or offend, but that is not the end in itself; those responses involve the audience so totally that there is an immediate emotional reaction to what they see, through being reached in the most sensitive area—our sexual privacies.

I am against all forms of censorship. Most people have greater personal concern about whether a man makes love to his cow than whether he goes to war and slaughters his current enemy. We have more laws against nudity than against guns, but that's because we still feel we have to pay the price for the original sin rather than face the ones we commit every day. It's easy to persecute something called nude theater, but why can't we accept it as another form of human communication presented on the stage, however directly?

Sex in the theater is a language that is so fine and subtle that the most delicate nuance, as well as the boldest statement, can be understood on both an emotional and an intellectual level. Each sexual act makes a different comment. By literally showing masturbation, fellatio, or fornication we can project abstract attitudes. Confronting the audience with flesh in action elicits an immediate response. How it is controlled measures the level of art it achieves.

Since the total sex act had never been presented on stage before, we expected difficulty in getting actors. The son of King Kong was a special problem because actors sometimes think that the part you offer them is a reflection of what you really think of them as human beings. After some had committed themselves to the various roles, they withdrew before the start of rehearsals. Finally, we found a cast that believed in what we were doing. The more they read the script, in the presence of the director and myself, the more they saw that there was no exploitation involved. What happened was that an extreme closeness developed between all of us, and everyone realized that all of the sexuality was required to underline the dialogue. The actors were absolutely free to touch, to make love. There was no difficulty in getting them to take their clothes off and to perform because we all felt we were working toward something beautiful. The only obstacle we anticipated was that of their being intimidated before an audience, but gradually the actors were so integrated into the play that their own inhibitions were submerged into the characters they were playing.

A week before we opened for previews, Ed Wode and I knew we would be a hit. The very first night of previews we had to turn away about one hundred people because the theater seated only 150. I have been accused of raping the box office and of having written and produced *Che!* as a publicity hoax that barraged the public. In truth, the only ad we took out was in *The Village Voice,* and the word-of-mouth campaign skyrocketed mainly because of my position in the Underground culture. I spent 1968 writing and editing for *The East Village Other* and similar publications, so naturally, when I had a play done, I was the center of focus among people connected with WBAI, WFMU, *The Realist, Screw, Rat, The New York Review of SEX,* the Fugs and others, like myself, who are trying to release the public from primitive taboos.

Opening night, we set the tone for the play by having the President and his cohort, Mayfang, picked up, driven around town, and delivered to the theater by a chauffeured limousine in keeping with the status of their characters. They walked through the lobby of milling first nighters and created quite a furore because, except for his top hat and a sash around his waist, he was stark naked, and she was wearing a silver suit with clear plastic cups showing her breasts and a Brillo pad over her pubic hair.

Audience reaction is not my particular concern since I believe that good entertainment must be destructive. Shaking people up is what my kind of theater is all about. If some

people are so upset that they walk out during the performance, at least I have made them think. On opening night a
picture was taken at an angle from the apron stage which
showed eight faces in the front of the audience. Only one person was looking directly at the President's penis, another had
one hand over his eyes, one had his head turned away, and a
woman had a quizzical expression on her face. I think, when
they got home, all of them, whether they stared or avoided the
issue, were haunted by the image.

Off Broadway and Off Off Broadway have the most enlightened and hip theater audience. Most of the times we found
them to be cool, but some of the nights they were very greedy,
trying to draw all the energy from the actors by wanting too
much.

On the second night David Merrick came down. We put him
in the hot seat which involved him in the play by having the
Sister of Mercy threaten to shoot off his penis. When she
lunged, he recoiled. At the end of the play, he applauded and
commented to a friend of mine, "It's a good way to make
money."

On the third night we got busted. This surprised us because
on that very day *The New York Times* carried a story about us
in which Deputy Inspector Fink said that he didn't think that
the play went against community standards, and he couldn't
decide, and not even the Supreme Court could decide, whether
it was obscene. After all, we weren't letting minors in, and it
was being performed in a theater, not the streets—the streets
are too polluted for that sort of thing; it's not even safe for
dogs to screw there. Suddenly after the show, the cops walked
in. There were about ten of them, and we were arrested on a
complaint made by Deputy Inspector Pine of the Public Morals Squad. They took us down to the Ninth Precinct, and we
spent the night in jail. The next day we were taken to court in
handcuffs—the director, the cast, myself, and a sixteen-year-

old boy who ran the mimeo machine (the charges against him were eventually dropped). The obscenities that were hurled at us by the police were worse than anything we were charged with. The decadence of the dungeons was more shocking than anything I could portray onstage. It took five hundred dollars bail apiece to get us out.

When David Merrick was approached to help us, he arranged for a special program on Channel 5 in which he said that *Che!* went too far, and that the actors stunk so much he had to put his handkerchief to his nose.

We called a press conference of our own at the theater and put on an actual performance of the play as it was originally presented. Since we had become a *cause célèbre* by this time, the audience was packed with correspondents from all the media and from as far away as Japan, Australia, Pago Pago, and Washington.

The next day we tried to get an injunction against the police so that they wouldn't harass us. We felt that they had no right to act as censors, and it should be up to the courts to decide whether we were guilty of any violations. The Dramatists' Guild and the Authors League sent telegrams to Mayor Lindsay to this effect. The judge ruled against us, and we were closed for a few weeks. Then one day we held another press conference at Sardi's and announced that we were going to open that night. Two weeks later the grand-jury indictment came down, which accused us of sexual war crimes committed during rehearsals, previews, opening night, and the first press conference, and we were busted again that night.

Prior to this Public Morals Squad arrest, I would read the obscene charges to the audience after each performance. They would roar at the technical descriptions. The President was accused of unsuccessfully trying to blow himself, and all were accused of conspiring to help him perform the act. This double whammy hit us on all counts from the Sister of

Mercy touching her breasts to the President's simulation of defecation. We were also all involved in Che gyrating his hips in such a way that it caused his penis to move in a lewd motion. Mayfang touching the President's anus with a plastic dildo made us criminals. That prop along with our scripts and reservation book were taken as evidence against us.

The second arrest was most peculiar. Inspector Pine had a ten-dollar seat but refused to sit there and made a big scene about preferring the six-dollar section on the side. At the end of the show, before the audience walked out, he jumped onstage and announced that Che, the President, and the Sister of Mercy were under arrest. The audience screamed in protest and were threatened by the police with arrest unless they left the theater. Police were everywhere to make sure that they obeyed. I was in the dressing room when they got me, too. This time we had to pay a thousand dollars bail, but we opened the next night and kept running.

Apart from what went on onstage, I believe that the reasons we were being persecuted were the political viewpoint of the play and the fact that we didn't have big money behind us. The question of our socially redeeming value affects the future of many other shows.

One night before our second arrest two policewomen and two detectives came to see the play, and they were all drunk. They sat in the first row and were sharing a bottle of gin and had a bag of ice which broke and spilled all over the place. When the play ended, one of the detectives went onstage and drank water from the President's toilet bowl. They resisted us trying to put them out, and we had to call the police ourselves to take them away, but we didn't press charges.

Critics, too, were troublesome. They refused to deal with the play, and misrepresented it because they came to the theater with their sexual biases. *Che!* is the perfect target for the lazy critic. He can deal with the nudity. He can talk about the erec-

Che! with Maryonne Shelley and Paul Georgiou
(Photograph by Charmian Reading)

tions and about whether the intercourse scene was well orches-
trated, and he doesn't have to contend with the ideas of the
play. The most perceptive reviews were done by such papers as
*The Village Voice, The Los Angeles Free Press, Rat, Christi-
anity and Crisis*, and *The East Village Other*, because they
were able to see the sexual aspects in their proper perspective. Every phase of American life from advertisements selling
coffins to miniskirted grandmothers has propelled sex to our
national consciousness. The Underground press digging *Che!*
reinforced the idea that the absence of sexual hangups is the
initial step to complete physical fullness, the "togetherness"
everyone is always talking about. If you're at ease with your
sexuality, no matter who you are or what you want to become, then you're at ease with everything. The hypocrisy that
sex evokes made one critic of a leading magazine come to all
the previews, and after watching what was happening—completely mesmerized—ask me to arrange an introduction to
Mayfang. I refused, and his review read, "If this play never
reopens, it will be a boon to untold thousands." My response
was to quote him out of context in an advertisement in *The
East Village Other:* "A boon to untold thousands."

The notoriety naturally helped build our following. With
audience participation, however, as it is today, we tried to
insure the President's penis for one million dollars but had to
settle for a $300,000 coverage.

Later we expanded the show to include more characters as
well as music and lyrics to widen the magical experience.

I have added to the cycle of sex and politics plays, of which
Che! is a part. There is now one about Farouk which deals
with the Middle East situation in which the Jews and the
Arabs are in a harem, another is *Rockefeller,* about the disap-
pearance of Michael Rockefeller in New Guinea, and one
called *Lumumba,* about the Congo and the U.N. as well as the
rest of Africa. There's also a play about the whole Hitlerian

episode. In that one I tried to show how perversion can turn against you when outside values force repression, and how furtiveness can destroy. If no one is interested in producing them, I will.

I'm continuing to teach psychology and American literature at the University of Rhode Island and to lecture on the theater at The City College of New York and the College of St. Thomas at St. Paul, Minnesota, as well as to write novels, poetry, and plays, and to work for national magazines and Underground newspapers. I don't want to get involved with an abstract movement. What happened to me is just one isolated incident in the general cause of complete freedom—the freedom to love our own bodies and the freedom to love anyone. The havoc that I've aroused was because I used the medium of sex to make people aware of their responsibilities to what is going on in the world today. I am amazed at the hostility that I've evoked. I have risked prison—and my cast and I have been fined—but I am glad that I have countered the prejudices that have dictated the limit to which an artist may express himself through the symbolism of sex.

X

The Experts in Conversational Excerpts: The New Broadway

BROOKS ATKINSON
formerly of *The New York Times*

THE ASSUMPTION that Off Broadway began after World War II confuses me, because when I first came to New York in 1922, that kind of theater was familiar and standard. I knew about it, even though I didn't become a critic until 1925. One of the first things I saw when I arrived in the city was an O'Neill play at the Provincetown Playhouse, a theater that had a romantic feeling about it, despite or because of the fact that it was converted from a stable. The seats were the most uncomfortable benches in the world, and the stage facilities were minus zero. The whole thing was very impromptu and impoverished, but I remember the play vividly, the *S. S. Glencairn* series with Walter Abel. That was about fifty years ago, so you can see Off Broadway made an impression on me even then.

The critics, I believe, covered the O'Neill plays Off Broadway, especially George Jean Nathan who admired him so. When I became a critic, it was standard practice to go to the Provincetown and Greenwich Village theaters. Before that, when I was editor of the book-review section, I remember going to see *Desire Under the Elms* at the Greenwich Village Theatre, a thrilling event, particularly since the incest theme gave the play a scandalous reputation. It was so shocking that it sent a tremor of pleasure throughout New York and caused the play to be moved up to Times Square. It had a long run—because the public thought it was pornographic not because it was art. I, personally, think it is the greatest of the O'Neill plays.

We also went to the Neighborhood Playhouse. We didn't think of places like that in terms of Off Broadway. We just considered them as where the action was. There were new and provocative things done, but also a lot of terrible stuff.

The first review I wrote for the *Times* was for the opening of the Cherry Lane Theatre. Although I was not the critic for the *Times,* I was asked to cover the event. I thought it was very bohemian to go to those grubby little places that didn't have the overwhelming style of the Broadway theaters. This was where things were happening!

I lived in the Village then, and I used to go to the small theaters, not only because it was more convenient, but also because it was what we called *experimental* theater. That big word was the holy term at that time. The audience was made up of cultivated people interested in the arts, and not ordinary people in search of entertainment.

I first met Eugene O'Neill about the time *Desire Under the Elms* was being done downtown, and I got to know him pretty well. As far as I'm concerned, relations between critics and authors, and critics and actors, are strained. I always felt uncomfortable, when I was reviewing, to meet people I had to write about. I'm sure they must have felt the same way. So I never assumed friendly associations with people in the theater.

When I ran into O'Neill on Broadway in 1933, I knew that he was going to produce a play based on Greek classics, *Mourning Becomes Electra.* I asked whether, in order to be prepared to review the play properly, I should do some research into the tragedies on which his was based.

He said, "No, you shouldn't do that. You should read the manuscript."

I felt that was strictly unethical, because a reviewer should walk into the theater like a member of the audience and not go in like a theater person. Even though I had never read a manuscript in advance, I didn't want to seem sanctimonious by telling him, "I'm too pure to do this kind of thing." So, I said, "Yes," and I read them.

In those days *Mourning Becomes Electra* was three separate plays, and the idea was to mount them on three consecutive nights—Monday, Tuesday, and Wednesday, then Thursday, Friday, and Saturday. My initial reaction was that the first play was great, the second was bad, and the third was better than the second but not as good as the first. I checked my opinion by reading them a second time. O'Neill was getting impatient at my keeping the manuscript so long. When I returned it and gave him my report, he was very upset. At that time I was living in the Catskills and he was living in Northport, Long Island, and he asked me to come to spend a weekend to talk things over. When I did, I could see that he was not the least bit interested in my opinion or anybody else's; he knew what he was doing and didn't give a damn what anyone said.

On going into production with the plays, they found it was physically impossible to do three separate plays, because it was too big a job and the actors couldn't memorize that much. So they cut them all and made one long play, which was superb.

In the thirties we didn't cover all the small theaters, because so many of them didn't seem worthwhile, but we particularly went to the political plays that were breaking out everywhere in what we called the Socially Conscious Theatre. The Civic Repertory had a left-wing Sunday night, and it was there that I first saw the sensational *Waiting for Lefty.*
I was away for four years during the war, so I don't know what went on in the theater during that period. My next recollection of Off Broadway is the 1952 Circle in the Square production of *Summer and Smoke.* People refer to that as the turning point of Off Broadway. I am not aware that it was, and, in fact, I wonder if it really was. I went there opening night, because I had seen the first production of the play in Dallas in 1947 and again when it was brought to Broadway and failed. I had always liked it. Unfortunately, it was produced on Broadway after *A Streetcar Named Desire*, and

people thought it was repetitious. I didn't think so. It had been written before *Streetcar.*

The Circle in the Square already had had one production, *Dark of the Moon,* which I did not go to but which I had in the back of my mind that I should have attended. When they had *Summer and Smoke,* I knew I had to go. I thought the production was excellent, and so did the public. Perhaps the intimacy of the playhouse helped a lot. There were not many seats, and you sat all around, which made it very sociable and established an ideal relationship between the actors and the audience. The informality and spontaneity gave just the right atmosphere for *Summer and Smoke.*

That was the first time I saw Geraldine Page, and she was exactly right for the part. I don't remember that there was anything magical about her. I thought she was extremely good and as it turned out to be, she's now great—but I can't say I saw this then, because I don't think I had the insight to see what she was going to become. I never had that kind of foresight about anybody.

Recently, a neighbor told me that she had heard on TV that I had discovered Geraldine. I said, "I remember reviewing her and that I wrote she was fine, but the idea that I found her and set her on the track to stardom is ridiculous." When my neighbor said, "Shame on you," all I could reply was, "I'm glad I didn't knock her."

Covering Off Broadway in the fifties was not a question of supporting it, but simply because a newspaper has to be where interesting things are going on. The Circle in the Square was the best of the groups in those days, and with its continuous management, it still is. Again, their surroundings and the relationship between audience and actor helped another Broadway failure, *The Iceman Cometh.*

I did have different standards when I went downtown, but it wasn't done with a slide rule. If you walk into a small tawdry theater, where you are only five feet away from the actors, you are naturally in a different frame of mind than when you go to Broadway. The proscenium stage sets up a conflict between actors and audience, and you wonder who's going to win the contest. I don't like the proscenium stage, and when I go to places like the Circle, I feel more with it than I do on Broadway. So, although I never consciously adjusted my standards, I know I did it unconsciously . . . inside the theater.

I didn't go to *Oh! Calcutta!* because it sounded like a hell of a chore getting in. I'm not that interested in nudity. I'm a champion of the nudeless theater. No nudes is good nudes in my book.

I felt out of it when I saw Grotowski, because I don't speak Polish, and I didn't know what was going on. The program had a very elaborate description of what was happening, but I was unable to follow it in my mind as it went along. I thought it was very interesting, but it reminded me of Meyerhold in Moscow in 1936 when I went there the first time. The actors were good, and it was vivid. But my way of deciding whether I like a thing or not is by feeling moved and personally involved. I never felt that about Grotowski. I ran into a Polish woman I knew, and she was enthusiastic. I guess understanding the language made the difference.

There was a time when I used to insist on the distinction between being called a reviewer and a critic. Everybody uses the term "critic." Reviewing is going to the theater as a member of the public to write a report for a newspaper on what happened. Of course, this is subjective, unlike the objectivity of other forms of newspaper writing.

A critic reads scripts and knows something about rehearsals and things like that. He looks at a play from a more thoroughly analytical frame of mind. He could also perhaps be fighting for a certain kind of theater. Maybe, like Shaw, he could have a political attitude toward the theater which he is promoting. I regard criticism as much more profound, judicial, and long-term than reviewing, which is done quickly. I hope I'm not underestimating reviewing, but its function is to provide news for people who are interested in the theater. As a reviewer, I didn't read plays nor follow out-of-town notices. I always tried to go into the theater like a member of the public and have only the public interest in what was going on.

It was very inconvenient covering Off Broadway when you had to get back to the newspaper to write your review that night. Once, when the Circle was doing *The Balcony,* Ted Mann hired a limousine to get us all back in time, because the city was immobilized by a heavy snowfall. I came into the *Times'* office late, saying, "I can't make the edition tonight, boys." But there is some compulsion about making it, and I did make the deadline all right.

In the beginning I used to make the second edition, which meant that after I got out of the theater about eleven, I had until one-thirty to write my review. But then, as the paper got more tightly organized, it came to the point where the review had to be done by twelve o'clock.

The five-hour O'Neill *The Iceman Cometh* opened on Broadway in the afternoon, so that we could get out at ten o'clock. That gave me another hour to write my notice. The next day, Terry Helburn of the Guild called me to say how pleased they were by what I'd written. I said, "Did you notice that all the reviews were good? Do you know why? It's because we had an extra hour." That was the beginning of the early curtain.

Unfortunately, the earlier we got out of the theater, the earlier the papers went to press, so we could gain a little time at the theater, and we would lose a little time at the office. It got so that, finally, I would get to the office at 10:45 and would have until 11:45 to get my thoughts down on paper. That gave me another ten or fifteen minutes to correct the proofs.

A man should know, when a play is over, whether he has enjoyed it or not. It's as simple as that. A reviewer has to present reasons why he feels as he does and has to be a little more analytical, perhaps, than the average theatergoer, but the basic decision whether the play is good or bad is easy for anybody to make, based on the kind of time he has had.

(Photograph by *The New York Times* Studio)

CLIVE BARNES
The New York Times

GOING OFF Broadway and Off Off Broadway regularly for the first time, when I became drama critic for *The New York Times,* completely changed my mind about the possibilities of the theater in America. I realized how much activity there was and how fundamentally good it was. Expenses are so high on Broadway that they have to play to the lowest common denominator kind of audience. You don't always have to be good, but you always have to be popular. Admittedly, Broadway does do some things marvelously, but lately it seems to me that most of the things that are really good have come from somewhere else. Broadway might be a great showcase, but it seems to have lost the power to really create anything.

Now, for the first time, you find some people even working Off Broadway for money. Look at *Boys in the Band,* which certainly has made Mart Crowley as much money as he would have made on Broadway. In the last few years Off Broadway has had two or three money hits, even though these still remain the exception and actors continue to be underpaid.

Critics are more concerned with influence than power. I became a critic because, while I had no creative talent, I had a great interest in the arts and a certain analytical ability. Being a critic has its value in providing a bridge between the artist and the audience. Not only does he help interpret a play, but he also provides the cheapest form of publicity the artist is ever going to get. A critic probably has more power Off Broadway than on, because certain built-in commercial factors, such as a popular star, can save a show uptown.

Off-Broadway theater—and even more Off Off-Broadway theater—explains the greater creativity of New York theater compared with London. The West End is often full of American imports, and most of the creative work is being done by the National Theatre, the Royal Shakespeare Company, and in the Royal Court Theatre, all heavily subsidized. Admittedly, London's level of acting and staging is higher than in New York. You cannot equate the London establishment organizations with the Broadway theater, and there is still no equivalent to Off Broadway.

British television is one reason for the difference between New York and London theater. It's so much better than American television that it is actually an enrichment of life. They do have some of the same awful serials and games we have here, but they also have original plays—something that's all but disappeared from the American scene. This offers so many opportunities for the playwright, since they do hundreds of plays a year, that some of the best ones get obsessed with the medium and stay there. They cease to think in terms of the theater. Another aspect of British TV and British films is that, like the theater, they are centered in London. An American actor has to choose between relative poverty in New York or relative affluence in L.A. The English actor has no such choice to make.

My critical standards are not different for a Broadway or an Off-Broadway show, but the same fair review that I give for an uptown show would make it run Off Broadway, especially if the word-of-mouth is good.

When you write a review, you can't really think of your readers, because you don't know who your readers are. They vary so much in taste, and once you start thinking of them, you're in the position of a man taking a poll. You can only say what you yourself think, and only when you feel that you may have some particular prejudice can you account to your readers.

I think it's reasonable to make intelligent allowances for certain things Off Broadway, such as what could be done if there had been more money. But when you make such excuses, your readers ought to know about it.

I once said that the American drama was *Waiting for Lefty* while everyone else was *Waiting for Godot*. Until now, it was out of the mainstream of art generally. At present, however, the new playwrights working Off and Off Off Broadway are trying to advance the theater in fresh ways, exploring original techniques. Today the movies are perhaps having a similar effect on drama that photography had on painting. The movies are liberating the theater. Now we are even questioning what exactly constitutes an evening in the theater. We wonder whether a play has to have a beginning, middle, and end, whether it needs a story at all, and in some instances whether it needs actors in the old sense. Such new departures could lead to "another" theater that would not make the present theatrical form redundant but could coexist with it.

(Photograph by *The New York Times* Studio)

WALTER KERR
The Sunday New York Times

THERE WAS no regular Off-Broadway reviewing when I joined the *Herald-Tribune* in 1961. Within six years, however, we were so busy covering the scene that we had to use second stringers and divide up the work. All the interest started with Brooks Atkinson's coverage of *Summer and Smoke.*

The same standard applies on or Off Broadway, and it's a pretty strict one. There may be a tinier or tackier set; we understand that. Everything depends upon the quality of the performance. No pluses are given for good intentions or noble aspirations. Productions are not differentiated as commercial or theatrical. Normally, a very good play will be commercial, provided that the reviewers admire its qualities and say so enthusiastically enough.

If you're on a major daily, you're presumably being read by a cross-section of people, some of whom buy *The Village Voice* and those who wouldn't be caught dead with it. You may not be influenced in your content, but your style of expressing yourself, when you write for the general reader, is such that any reasonably intelligent person who picks up the paper should be able to understand what you're talking about.

I've enjoyed dozens of exciting discoveries Off Broadway. I was particularly pleased the night I came across Murray Schisgal, because he made me laugh so much and so hard at material that some observers might think was done to death, but I thought that he kept ahead of. When I saw Jason Robards playing *The Iceman Cometh* for the first time, I thought what a powerful performance that really was! I remember Joseph Anthony, who had been an actor, directing *Bullfight,* and I thought there's a director we can use. Joseph

Hardy, who did *You're a Good Man, Charlie Brown* Off Broadway, is a fine director. His *Johnny No Trump* on Broadway was a superb job of putting a play together and making actors refresh themselves. He now has the recognition he deserves.

Off Broadway has become financially viable because of the quality and increased popularity of things being done there. People are beating down the doors trying to get into some of the shows, and are willing to pay fifteen dollars a seat. Now that this has happened, Off Broadway runs the risk of getting as commercial as Broadway. It is now becoming the new Broadway.

There are a lot of plays that might as well be done downtown at the least possible expense. I'm not in favor of massive productions, and I think it is one of the big problems of the Broadway theater. The cost of operation makes shows close more quickly. I'm interested in text and in acting, and I don't care about things like decor which cost money. Shows like *Boys in the Band,* which look so polished that you don't have to make excuses for them, make Off Broadway the commercially possible Broadway. I can't let it dismay me that this process has taken place. Being put into the position where momentary success as its objective will create new problems for Off Broadway while it solves some old ones. The theater is moving in that direction, because we can't afford Broadway costs anymore, and Off Broadway will have to go Off Off and after that Off Off Off—there's no end to it.

The best ensemble work I've seen in recent years has been in *The Boys in the Band* and *No Place to Be Somebody.* Both companies were impeccable and brought to an equal pitch. I don't think I've seen better companies on Broadway. I like Broadway's level of competence, and I think they're trying to do good work there. The fact that it does badly so much of the time is really nothing to hold against it. Experiments fail, too, Off Broadway, so it's not surprising that conventional plays should.

So much is being done Off Off Broadway that you can't possibly keep up with it. If you hear a great deal about a particular production, you try to catch it.

Joseph Chaikin's Open Theatre production of *The Serpent* is the best example of collaborative and improvised theater I've seen. The actors worked in the laboratory with the writer, Jean-Claude van Itallie, before bringing it to Off Broadway. The text amounts to one quarter of what an ordinary script would be in playing time. The rest is mime which is worked out on the floor with the director and actors, as well as the writer. It's absolutely fascinating to watch Cain try to kill Abel since no one had ever killed anyone else before.

Nontext plays are a phase we have to go through, though I have to admit it bothers me. I'm a text man, but I don't think it is the beginning and the end. I believe that the machinery originally came from a body making gestures and doing things on the stage, using a voice or perhaps not. Those actors improvised what they spoke, and every time they landed a good line, they probably remembered it and used it again until it hardened through performance. This active will of the theater grew and became more complex, then it reached for the organized word. That kind of word can dig deeper and have greater penetration. The control that is exerted by the writer has resulted in richer works. I don't want to remand that, but I do see some sense in stopping briefly to reexamine all the elements of the theater. It may shake up some of the thinking we do about the texts, and that is good because texts have been getting lazy, conventional, and familiar. I imagine, though, we will return to the text because it's a more complex form of the theater.

I've always hated the idea of the fourth wall, which was something that came with naturalism, but the box set where actors ignored you all night has existed only for a limited time in the history of the theater. Prior to the nineteenth century, actors were playing right at you, and the audience was more drawn into the experience. We need to forget the photographic idea and relate ourselves to the performers. Some of the experiments that have been going on Off and Off Off Broadway push the interchange beyond what it will tolerate and will collapse as a result. I'm perfectly willing to undergo the attempts and even endure the bad ones to see where the borderline is that we've lost.

Grotowski can have me sitting within the set with actors crawling all over me, but since they are most clearly acting, it doesn't bother me a bit, and in some way they put me at my ease. I know that they are not going to violate my public privacy. With the Living Theatre, however, I have a feeling that they claimed an unearned intimacy. They came up to me, screamed at me, pointed at me, and touched me—and I didn't ask them to. Being approached without an invitation from me, makes me feel more detached.

The important thing with Grotowski's actors is that they always remain actors. They have a steady distance that maintains their standards as performers. I am opposed to violent participation, just as I dislike asking the audience to write or act half the play for the simple reason that we are not likely to be good writers or actors. Also, it makes me apprehensive because I feel most alone and fragmented in the theater when I see an actor heading in my direction.

Joseph Chaikin, with his experiments in this area, is honest

enough to know how audiences feel about this sort of thing.
We can only find where the boundary is by trying.

I expect to see Off Broadway becoming more money minded.
It's the natural operation of things, and it's all right, because
we need a financially solvent alternative to Broadway to bring
prices and production costs down. That will happen if we
spread out the work a little more. The greater the demand for
Off Broadway, and the higher its prices, the slicker it's going
to become. That doesn't worry me because Off Off Broadway
will then provide the experimental space.

One thing about this nudity thing is that people look more
alike when they're undressed. You don't realize that until you
see it, but you've got a lot more similar skin to look at when
the entire body is shown. I went to see a rock musical called
Salvation and was very much taken with a young actress who
was not nude. I looked at her credits and discovered that she
had been in *Oh! Calcutta!,* but I'd never noticed her. When
you wear clothes, you direct attention to the face, and that's
where the personality is, especially around the eyes and
mouth. It doesn't come from out of your left elbow or from
the tint of your skin. Clothes actually help you to know somebody.

When I first went to the *Herald-Tribune* fifteen years ago,
there were seven newspapers, now there are three. If you have
seven papers, you could get mixed press on a show and still
have a chance, but with three papers it's pretty set. To add one
more voice to daily criticism, I decided to do my column
weekly. Another reason for that switch is that after so many

years of daily reviewing, I wanted a new perspective, to stand back and look without having to devote my energy to the one particular thing I was covering tonight. And if I could make "tonight" not seem so important, I wondered if I could see more. I like the situation as it is now, but there have been some gains and some losses. I'm not sure how much value that extra vote has been yet, because it comes so late. In London it's easier, because the weekly sentiments come out the same week as the daily notices, and the public sees the whole package. Here we go to press so much earlier that they come out a whole week later, and the Sunday notice does not seem a part of the general critique. Even though I may not have been as much help as I had hoped, I enjoy it more this way.

The audience is starting to get choosy, in a box-office sense, Off Broadway, too. It's not responding to everything just because of good notices. People are operating on a "Do I think I'll like it" premise—the hunch-basis that dictates Broadway theatergoing so much. The subject matter is playing a more important part Off Broadway. The public is getting harder to sell since there are more productions competing.

Reviewers, generally speaking, have been pretty strict with Off Broadway. As far as Off Off Broadway is concerned, I may have seen things that were weak, or not inventive enough, but I would never call it amateurish.

JERRY TALLMER
The New York Post

THE SEVEN years I was the Off-Broadway drama critic for *The Village Voice*—from 1955 to 1962—my career coincided with the Off-Broadway boom, and they needed us for publicity. It was Julie Bovasso's production of *The Maids* that brought me into that world.

I thought there should be some kind of rewards for Off Broadway, and that's how the Obie came into being. We had three judges then, but now it's up to five—but I think three was the right number—and it's a majority decision.

When Jack Gelber's *The Connection* opened in the summer of 1957, it was totally ignored and would have died but for a piece I wrote in the *Voice* praying that it would stay alive. People began coming down, including Kenneth Tynan who was then writing for *The New Yorker* and Robert Brustein who was on *The New Republic*. I think it was one of the turning points in modern American theatergoing, because it broke down that false fourth wall. The way it involved the audience was a big push for the avant-garde.

The Living Theatre that returned from Europe was entirely different, and a much less superior thing than they used to be when they made that breakthrough. Though I did like a few things in their production of *Frankenstein,* most of their new attempts were basically irresponsible.

I can't stand this idea of familiarity and touching the audience. They are not devices that actually involve people, at least not me; they actually turn me off. I know about the theory of the theater of cruelty, but it just doesn't work. Even when the Living Theatre had their actors, still in character, beg during the intermission of *The Connection*, I thought it was a little

(*New York Post* photograph by Jacobellis © 1971, New York Post Corporation)

silly and had to discard that when I went back in to see the rest of the play.

I don't know how to say what theater is except when I see it. When I see theater and it excites me, I know it and want to write about it. Theater has nothing to do with whether or not some actor is sitting in my hip pocket or crying into my ears; it has to do with ideas, writing, acting, staging, meaning, important truth, and a number of other things. A beautiful production of *The Three Sisters* from twenty feet away with everybody being very precise gets me and a lot of other sensible people more involved than sitting around some little loft with actors crawling over and under me, representing our sick society or whatever the hell else they do.

A critic has to think of his readership. Your evaluations may be the same, but the way you state them changes according to the paper you're writing for. The specialized audience of over 100,000 of *The Village Voice* want things said a different way than the 750,000 that read a family newspaper like the New York *Post*.

Off Off Broadway has been tremendously important in finding the latest group of young American playwrights. Whether any of them will be significant, no one can say. I also see a great deal of bilge and pseudo avant-garde nonsense in those theaters. Though it grates my teeth, there are critics, especially the current crop on the *Voice,* who like that stuff much more than I do. I've pretty much had my fill of it. It has nothing to do with the generation gap, only artistic irresponsibility.

Ellen Stewart's La Mama has shaken us all up and brought in some quite interesting shows, but groups like that are so open that they allow for semiprofessionalism and lots of running around and yelling.

One of the functions of a critic is to encourage, though I do discourage when I have to. I've seen a lot of things Off Broadway that I loved cut down by other critics. It may sound corny, but once in a while you may be the only one to praise someone or something in print, then you get a letter telling how much you've helped.

Originally a great many people worked Off Broadway simply to get on Broadway, and while I don't think it's a bad objective, you should be honest about it. The Circle in the Square built an entire reputation doing a different kind of thing downtown, and as soon as they got ten dollars in the bank, they rushed uptown. It's unfair to pretend that your soul is pure and your heart is clean, when you really want to become a Broadway producer. The Living Theatre would never do that. Once you claim that you reject crass materialism, and then make a jump for it, that qualifies as being suspect. For playwrights and actors Off Off Broadway should feed Off and Off Broadway should on, but there are some people who have pretended that their minds are set on a certain objective whereas all along they were eyeing something else. Those who get rich Off Broadway are the worst kind of hustlers.

There's an old saying that you always go to the theater with hope, and you leave ready to commit suicide. Once in a while you enter with no expectations and come out overjoyed. That only happens maybe once or twice a year.

There have been occasional plays through the years which opened on Broadway and should never have done so. They were not cut to the cloth of the Broadway audience, and they died too soon. Some lingered on, but I don't know whether they made any money. They would have made a better impact Off Broadway. One such production that I fondly remember was *Look, We've Come Through.* It was a beautiful play, and many people I've met since also thought so. It just couldn't be understood on Broadway, by either the critics or the public, and it closed within a week or two. I begged its director, José Quintero, to move it right down to Off Broadway. He wanted to, but Equity has rules against that, and there would have been a long waiting period—by then, anyway, nobody wanted to do it.

More important was the presentation of what I think is the greatest play of the twentieth century, *Waiting for Godot.* Michael Myerberg, its producer, insisted not only on having its American premiere at the Coconut Grove Theatre in Florida—where you can imagine how it went over—but also he insisted, and I suppose he will insist to this day, that it was right for Broadway. In a big ad he said he was looking for 70,000 intellectuals. He must have found them somehow, because the play ran for ten weeks, and Mr. Myerberg claims that he broke even.

To me, that was a distortion of the play, especially since the world mostly raved about Bert Lahr's performance. I am angry everytime there is a revival of *Godot* that gives greater emphasis to the playing than to the content of the play. There are millions of people who know how great that Nobel Prize winning work is through reading it. A few years ago I saw a production of it by the Free Southern Theatre, a fairly young interracial group who had the courage to go down to the deep South and tour tiny rural communities, where there were blacks and whites with no education who accepted the play quite well. They also performed it in New York City at the New School, where I caught it. Even though they weren't good as actors, they understood how to do it. They performed slowly and pointedly, but it came off better than any production of *Godot* I've ever seen.

Maybe someday there will be a place for that kind of play on Broadway, but if I were introducing Samuel Beckett to the United States of America for the first time, I would not pick a Broadway theater to do it in. The same goes for Brecht and Ionesco, simply because there aren't many people out there who want to go to that sort of thing. They just don't want to think. They're always being referred to as poor dumb audiences, but they ask for it as anybody who's ever been to a Broadway show knows.

Two other examples of shows that were done on Broadway and were well received by the critics, but didn't gain the audience were John Osborne's *The Entertainer* and *Epitaph for George Dillon*. They would have fared better had they opened Off Broadway.

We're getting closer to a dead-end street on Broadway. Maybe it will become just a theater for big, bouncy musicals—good, bad, or indifferent.

HAROLD CLURMAN

A L L M Y life I've been going to theater wherever it is. The Off-Broadway nomenclature hasn't really meant very much to me except as a reminder of the inconvenience of traveling downtown to theaters that are not always comfortable. But theater is theater, and where it is situated makes very little difference to me. As a matter of fact, my first job as an actor was Off Broadway in the Greenwich Village Theater run by O'Neill, Jones, and McGowan. Shortly after that, I went to their Provincetown Playhouse to work as a property man; I was probably the worst one in the history of the American theater.

Greenwich Village, in those days, had something bohemian about it. That isn't true anymore. Now it just seems impoverished and ragged. That isn't true of the productions, of course. In fact, they are too expensively produced now. Very often they put on the kind of shows that the big boys do and spend too much money on production and scenery when it's not necessary. One of the advantages of Off Broadway used to be that you could put on a show cheaply and attract an adventurous audience. Now everything seems so lavish and costs as much as a Broadway production did in 1935. This makes me skeptical about the whole venture and often it just turns out bad Broadway.

The Group Theatre of which I was the director during the Depression was interested in plays of social significance. We didn't go Off Broadway, because we wanted to appeal to a much larger audience. Besides, we were thoroughly professional and had a first-class company. We wanted to produce new playwrights. At that time theater tickets were so cheap— about three dollars for an orchestra seat—that we had no reason to go Off Broadway. Our belief in ourselves as a major effort was immediately justified by the attention and praise we attracted.

(Photograph by Friedman-Abeles)

Clifford Odets was a young writer we felt we should give a chance to. His *Waiting for Lefty* was done Off Broadway at a benefit performance at the Civic Repertory Theatre on 14th Street. It was done to win a contest for the best liberal play that could be performed without scenery for a working-class audience. Odets wrote it in a couple of nights while on the road with one of our shows. He used members of our company for its Off-Broadway premiere, and then did the show for the taxi drivers' union itself. We then brought it up to Broadway, where it got great notices and almost set off the whole left-theater movement in this country. As a matter of fact, it helped perpetuate the leftist image for the Group Theatre.

I tend to be lenient, wherever possible, with new art forms, and a little more permissive if it's done under obviously difficult technical circumstances—but on the whole, Off Broadway should be judged as we judge other things. I myself will very rarely write an adverse review of an Off-Broadway show. I would rather skip it, because I know the struggles of those working there. If it's a pretentious play and it's bad, I will say so. For that matter, I skip certain Broadway productions if I believe they are not worth discussion by adults. I enjoy this privilege because I write for a magazine, whereas newspaper critics have to cover everything. I don't consider my reviews news; I consider them criticism. By the time they hit the stand it's about a week after the play has opened. So whether it's a flop or not is already established.

I can write a review in an hour, but I wouldn't enjoy it, nor would I believe it serious criticism. It's okay if you want to say "great," "bad," or "lousy," but I like to give my writing more reflection.

I hate long reviews about unworthy plays. To go on for three paragraphs rapping an unimportant play is like trying to hit a fly with an atomic bomb. A play should have a certain level of dignity and be a big target if you attack it. The only people and plays I attack are the great stars and the great successes.

I still direct all over the world, but only once did I do an Off-Broadway show. That was several years ago in a theater on West 42nd Street. It was Anouilh's *Romeo and Jeanette,* a play that wasn't successful in either its Paris or London productions, and it failed here, too. I never liked the script much, but my then wife wanted to play the lead.

I tried to do the play economically, even though I had to have a set that had a pompous look. The cast wasn't bad, but I think I could have gotten better actors to play the parts if I could have paid more. I blame myself for not doing as good a job as I should have. It just happens, let us say. No one guarantees excellence in work or anything else. The truth is I didn't have much enthusiasm for the play. There was some satisfaction in knowing that Laurence Olivier didn't do much better with the play in London.

There are more interesting things Off Broadway now than on. We're so anxious for a play of merit that we sometimes give it greater attention than it deserves, particularly when it's Off Broadway. This is truer of the critics than of the audience.

MARTIN GOTTFRIED

AS FAR as I'm concerned, you'll find the same kind of actors, playwrights, producers, and directors Off Broadway as you do on. They cater to the same fifty-year-old intellectual mentality. The big problem is to reach the younger people who affect all the changes that are going on in this country now. Their thinking is reflected Off Off Broadway. Though it isn't so radical, at least there is a change which is more than I can say for Off Broadway. So I like to call Off Off Broadway a junior version of Off Broadway.

The difference between a reviewer and a critic is that a reviewer who wants to make himself superior to other reviewers calls himself a critic. The rule of thumb for reviewing is that you are responsible to a newspaper or magazine to cover all Equity productions. The idea being that, if it's Equity, it's professional—but we know that there are plenty of Equity productions that aren't professional and vice versa. As a result, non-Equity Off Off-Broadway productions are seldom reviewed. Of course, that is silly, but at the same time many of them claim to be experimental or laboratory productions, not really wanting to be covered—but you know what happens, when there's a chance of them being reviewed, they say they're ready. If you do review them, and you like them, they say they were prepared. If you don't, however, they say they were just experimenting. It's particularly difficult for a critic, since he has to cover three or four Equity openings a week and finds himself up against thirty or forty Off Off-Broadway lofts.

Criticism is terribly necessary to someone who's doing work. The playwright, director, and actors have no real way of know-

(Photograph by John Maguire)

ing what they did and whether it worked or not, unless they get an absolutely objective opinion. They're not going to get that from each other or from their friends. The only way they can get some perspective is from a theoretically ideal critic, one who is capable enough to see what it is they did, understand what they were trying to do, and tell them whether they did it.

There's more to catch Off Off Broadway than there ever was Off Broadway. The Judson still has some amateurism, but La Mama is more professional and is more adventurous than Off Broadway. Compared to three or four years ago, when La Mama presented the work of a lot of kids, La Mama is very smooth now, but some of the spirit is gone. I suppose the more professional you get, the more you develop your craft, the less you take chances. People are adventurous when they're struggling, when they're doing something for love, when they're real believers and not in it just to make money.

I never make allowances. I walk into a theater, no matter where it is, and judge what I see by its own standards. This is particularly true Off Off Broadway which is much more radical for our time than Off Broadway was for its. Since there is more dance movement and company creation than the words of playwrights, and this can be either beautifully disciplined or sloppy, it tests the latitude of the critic.

What will happen to actors who are developing in plays with little dialogue? Will they be able to act in more verbal plays? They say they don't care about that, but I don't know how they'll be able to graduate into the mainstream of theater.

Off Off Broadway has much more inbreeding than Off Broadway ever had. It seems like they're going to stay on their own home grounds and never go anywhere. You might say there's a kind of artistic fetishness in that environment. They do things for and about one another. I don't know why their playwrights don't grow, but they just don't seem to be able to. I don't mean that they have to become more conservative or wind up with a Broadway hit, but Broadway is where the major audience is. If playwrights don't move out of those lofts and work in the larger arena, I don't see how they have a chance of changing the tastes of American theatergoers.

One of our main problems is to get the ideas that are so prevalent among the young people now into the theater, not only for the theater's sake as a growing organism but also to develop the young audience. For them, attending the theater is like going to Radio City Music Hall. The movies reflect their mentality, and unless the theater does the same, it will never regain that audience and their children. There won't be anybody out there. Off Off Broadway—if it is the alternative theater I think it is—can help with that problem. My personal conflict is whether Off Off Broadway should have anything to do with Broadway, or should it be off on its own without worrying about feeding the mainstream.

I've found the most obscure theaters, in the most out-of-the-way places, and the fact that there are people there shows that our theater was never healthier. There's never been so much activity, so many participants, so many different ideas. Now there are really all kinds of theater.

XI
The Off Off-Broadway Theater:
HOWARD GREENBERGER
This Play on Our Future Has a Name

THE CIRCLE has been completed!

One Sunday evening in 1960, after drinks at the Plaza Hotel, I rushed downtown to meet some friends at the Caffè Cino at 31 Cornelia Street, between Bleecker and Fourth streets. This was our favorite coffeehouse, because the old shaving mugs used for serving were mighty and the owner, Joe Cino, was generous with the whipped cream on our cappuccino. What's more, the atmosphere was not as commercial as that of the other coffeehouses. We felt relaxed in this environment, which was saved from being downbeat by the provocative paintings on the brick walls. Even more so than usual I found its unpretentiousness appealing, having just come from the Plaza.

That night some of the small tables which were normally scattered around the storefronted, long, and narrow room had been rearranged, and a bank of them had been set up at the far end. My friends had already gotten a table, which was lucky since the place was packed—quite unusual for a coffeehouse off the MacDougal beat. The roundish figure of Joe Cino came forward to announce that this evening he was having some of his regular patrons read Truman Capote's "A Christmas Memory." This was a follow-up to his presentation of the Chamber Poets on Sunday nights, which had been going on for a few months. The difference this time, however, was that the readers were assuming characters rather than expounding poetry and that made it more of a theatrical event. So moving was the experience that I was embarrassed at the lights in the audience not being turned out to allow me to cry in private.

That performance is considered the beginning of Off Off Broadway. The Caffè Cino was not the only *théâtre intime* around then, but by putting on weekly shows—soon graduating to a full-scale dramatization of *Candide* with sixteen actors and to its first original play by Jim Howard—Joe Cino made *The Village Voice* give them recognition by designating this new movement Off Off Broadway and publishing regular announcements of productions.

(Photograph by Robert D. O'Connor)

After a decade in which Off Off Broadway moved from coterie obscurity to international fame, Cinderella was invited to the ball. The Caffè Cino's production of *Dames at Sea* played the Plaza—the in and the out have come around to each other!

Soon after that initial show, I found myself no longer a spectator but a participant in the Movement. A friend of mine, Daniel Haben Clark, was in desperate need of a director for a one-act play which was to open at the Cino within a couple of days—the original director having left for some forgotten reason. Knowing my writing and directing background in theater and television, he called me. With nothing to lose and fun and satisfaction to gain, I pitched in. For two days and nights, with a cast of four, including the author's talented sister Connie, we molded *The Singing Lesson* into shape. The entertainment of about a hundred people in two performances a night while they enjoyed their coffee and pastries was our objective—and that we did. None of the production people were paid, but the actors realized some recompense for their week's work by asking for donations. This was literally the Pass the Hat Theatre.

I still have an image of Joe Cino lurking somewhere in the dark during rehearsals and calling out for more spicing up because he knew what his customers wanted. Whatever it was he wanted, he was entitled to get, since he paid for the overhead on all the productions by working as a typist during the day. Even though some of the greatest Off Off-Broadway hits emerged from his coffeehouse, Joe Cino, until his suicide in 1967, never received any of the money or the glory that was to come from this new tributory theater he started.

Within only a couple of years, a multitude of novices on the fringes of professional theater followed the Cino's lead and set themselves up wherever they could find space—from lofts to basements, from churches to bars. This free-for-all theater, not under the jurisdiction of the union because no real admission was charged and Equity members were not supposed to appear (but often did under other names), resulted in untold numbers of such organizations, most of which didn't last long. The most prominent among the more than a hundred still in existence are the Judson Poet's Theater of Al Carmines, Ralph Cook's Theatre Genesis, the Extension, the Old Reliable, John Vaccaro's Playhouse of the Ridiculous, and Joseph Chaikin's Open Theatre.

Epitomizing all that Off Off Broadway stands for is La Mama Experimental Theatre Club, run by Ellen Stewart who, despite being a black woman designer from Louisiana and completely untrained in the theater, has become the figurehead in what its adherents like to call the New Theatre.

"It all began with this pushcart idea," Ellen will tell you in her geechee accent. It seems that at the start of the fifites, she arrived in New York, wanting to be a designer, and was desperate for a job. She went into a church, which turned out to be St. Patrick's Cathedral, lighted a candle, made a wish, and within twenty minutes found herself hired as a porter in the store across the street, Saks Fifth Avenue. On her days off, she would take a subway ride to wherever she felt like getting off. One Sunday she found herself on the Lower East Side and met a man who became like a father to her, Abraham Diamond, one of the first people to introduce pushcarts to the area. He supplied Ellen with fabrics with which to work up her own designs, and even more important, he gave her this philosophy: "Every human being should have a pushcart of his own, not to eat from himself but to feed others, in order to be self-sufficient."

The designs for her own clothes attracted so much attention that Ellen became an executive designer in the store where she had started only three months before as porter. Ten years of this and of free-lancing found Ellen in Tangiers, dissatisfied with her life. She was talking to a friend who also brought up the pushcart idea, and remembering "Papa" Diamond, Ellen realized what she had to do for her own fulfillment. She resolved to make a dream come true for her brother, Fred Lights, and his friend Paul Foster by building the theater these aspiring playwrights had always talked about.

Although her brother has never used Ellen's theater, Paul and hundreds of other writers, including myself, have benefited from her decision. At first, her idea was to do this in conjunction with a boutique at 321 East Ninth Street, but the shop was short-lived and the theater took over. On July 27, 1962, she opened with an adaptation of Tennessee Williams' short story, *One Arm*. The audience had to be solicited from passersby. It didn't take long, however, for this artistic outlet to become known throughout the Village.

Harassed for breaking building codes, Ellen had all the customers one night after the show carry the tables and chairs up Second Avenue to where she ran the new operation as a private club. Using her earnings as a designer, Ellen made this second-floor loft into a regular theater with a stage and offered coffee for a dollar—in addition to a one-act play. It was here that I first worked for La Mama.

Having a script I wanted to direct, Robert Reinhold's *Five Fitts*, I arranged an introduction to Ellen and immediately became one of her "little biddies"—a term she uses when she feels a "beep" about a person that makes her believe in him. She gave me a week for the show two months away, and helped me line up the composer, set designer, lighting man, and stage manager, all from the little book of devoted followers that she had accumulated in the last couple of years. Bob and I paid for all props and scenery which ran about $150.

I had no difficulty in getting Barbara Cason and Jerry Mickey, who have been on and Off Broadway, for the leads because by now the Café La Mama had become a desirable showcase for actors seeking further employment. Rehearsals were held in my home until the day before the performance when we hurriedly got the scenery up and had a couple of run-throughs at the theater. At no time was Ellen concerned about what was being presented and just desired to smooth over any difficulties. Otherwise, her only function during a performance was to greet the audience—as she still does—by ringing a cowbell and introducing the play with "Welcome to La Mama E.T.C., Experimental Theatre Club, dedicated to the playwright and all aspects of the theater." Then she would park herself on the steps outside the theater while the play was on. She had faith in you and showed it by not interfering. She made sure *The Village Voice* came down and basked in the praise they gave. My greatest feeling of achievement came one night when she was ready to make her usual exit before the show, and I saw her become so transfixed by the opening of the play that she stayed till the end, and then she gave me a hug afterward as only La Mama can.

Those were the days, in the midsixties, when the young people who were seeking new freedoms came to the La Mama because there were no holds barred. Nudity was introduced on the stage there. And the form of most plays was almost non-existent, not only because Ellen herself preferred the abstract but also because it seemed that most of her playwrights—either by choice or by inability—did not write well-constructed plays. To make this negative virtue work with mostly untrained actors, a new style of performing evolved, which was more reliant on the physical and less on the verbal means of communicating ideas. The group grope, improvisation, and audience participation became standard practice here, and as perfected by Tom O'Horgan, this style made its impact on Broadway a few years later with *Hair.* Back then, however, it had its appeal to the select few of La Mama devotees who were just learning to thumb their noses at the Establishment by fingering a few other things.

When Ellen was told that to get her writers published, critiques were needed, she arranged a European tour, with two directors and sixteen actors doing twenty-one plays by some of her outstanding alumni: Sam Sheppard, Paul Foster, Jean-Claude van Itallie, Lanford Wilson, and Adrienne Kennedy. So successful were they that branches of La Mama began in several European countries, and on their return *Six from La Mama* was presented in a not-too-well-received Off-Broadway production.

All this recognition still did not impress the police, fire, and building departments which kept bothering Ellen with technicalities. Having had enough of this, Ellen would have closed down here and opened up shop in Europe had not the Rockefeller and Ford Foundations come through with grants that allowed her to buy a building to house the La Mama, to pay the actors for performing, and to cover the cost of productions for up to one hundred dollars each.

Now with a reconverted factory that once had been an opera house at 74A East Fourth Street, off Second Avenue, the complexion of the La Mama has changed. There are two fully equipped theaters that are intentionally sparsely furnished and flexible in setup, a rehearsal floor that also serves for classes, and a top floor where Ellen lives, so she is always available.

Even more significant than the physical changes in the La Mama is the difference in the atmosphere. Every floor is throbbing with activity, topped off upstairs by the happenings in Ellen's office-home. Around her oak round table can be found theater celebrities of the caliber of Peter Brook and Jerzy Grotowski, as well as lesser-known lights from all over America and nearly every foreign country, all vying for Ellen's and each other's attention amidst an insistent barrage of phone calls from production people with problems and from groups that want to give Ellen another award to add to her collection. The air is laden with questions being asked by some magazine or out-of-town-newspaper reporter who has finally noticed the space the La Mama has been grabbing in *The Sunday New York Times* and has decided to catch up. Piercing through the general din are pointed remarks about the movie and Off-Broadway deals being made, Leonard Melfi's total acceptance by Sophia Loren-Carlo Ponti and the rest of the Rome crowd, what Sam Sheppard and the Open Theatre meant to Antonioni, and the similarity of Tom Eyen unto Mike Nichols and Elaine May. Conspicuously absent today are references to Tom O'Horgan with whom Ellen has had a rift and who is the only gift this playwright's theater has thus far been able to give to Broadway that would be accepted—a director! In his place, and in the place of so many of the *originals* (pun intended), are latecomers who only a few years ago would not have had the courage or the foresight to be associated with the likes of the La Mama until it gained approval—the hard way—of the fashionably intellectual set.

With too many claims on her time, Ellen brought in a business manager, Jules Weiss, who could be heard muttering that it would be better to keep the theater closed than to put on a play that might not attract full houses. Such an attitude screams out against everything the La Mama once stood for, before it burst on Broadway with Julie Bovasso and on Off Broadway with Tom Eyen's *The Dirtiest Show in Town*, and made its mark, however tiny, on movies with an adaptation of its greatest hit, *Futz,* and dazed television audiences with the electronic tricks of *Hans Kringler.* Back before all this put La Mama in its present elite niche, Ellen's greatest concern was to keep the theater open for the sake of the show under any circumstances, not considering herself a judge of quality but an instrument for presentation.

A memorable night that typified the old attitude was when we all pitched in to keep the old Café La Mama on Second Avenue from being put out of business by the fire department, which demanded an expensive repair. All of us who had been working down there put on *Bang!*—more than twenty acts, which raised the cash to keep things going and showed the spirit that was La Mama.

Adding to the tribulations of success is the constant intru-

Original production, *Our Play on the Future Has No Name*, with Helen
Hanft (in print dress) and members of the chorus (Photograph by
Robert D. O'Connor)

sion of strangers. Ellen's door will open, and an unfamiliar, nervous face will appear above a body that seems to be wrapped around an envelope, obviously containing a script. After a brief introduction—Ellen is always available to talk to anyone—the intruder will learn that at the La Mama, even though both theaters have new productions running every week, there are commitments at least six months in advance to proven playwrights, colleges, groups that need an outlet, and directors that want to experiment with classics, and that the uninitiated writer better begin elsewhere. No good leaving the script, either. There are too many unread ones around already—waiting.

God knows, Ellen is still giving her all and then some. I appreciate how she personally helped me in my most recent production down there. The show was *Our Play on the Future Has No Name,* a musical farce about the first Jewish astronaut on which I collaborated with Robert Reinhold. The music was by Charlie Cuva, direction by myself with the assistance of Don Price, and it starred the First Lady of Off Off Broadway, Helen Hanft. The results caused Brooks Atkinson to write, "What I liked was the vitality, the variety, the sardonic humor, and the fundamental good nature of the whole work."

The working conditions, however, put everyone on edge. Ellen did everything she could to lay the groundwork for getting this complicated production on. Yet her guiding spirit that brought us to her before was not there when we needed it.

One of the major functions of a producer is to bring the creative forces together in an atmosphere conducive to bringing about their best work. Ellen's major contribution had always been to elicit this from those who worked for free by making them feel so loved and appreciated that they would feel privileged to dedicate themselves to building a better theater. Instead, the result was a bigger one that requires too much of Ellen, particularly since there is also a drive to have an international reputation. This makes for a dispersal of energies and a flaccidity back home. The demands on her are too great, and she is always on the go.

When my show was to be presented, after a year's work, she was not there, being away in Europe on a tour with her troupe. Those she left in her stead were not free enough to accept this unusual musical which was conceived to challenge anyone with any kind of prejudice. I had to cope with being regarded as "too revolutionary" for the so-called revolutionary theater. Compounded with this was a sense of having to "make it" which was reinforced by having to sign away five percent of any returns I may in the future get from the show.

The future is what Ellen has spent all her time, money, and energies gambling on. That her hopes for such playwrights as Leonard Melfi, Israel Horowitz, Rochelle Owens, Maria Irene Fornes, Megan Terry, Julie Bovasso, Harry Katoukas, Paul Foster, and Sam Sheppard have not been realized in one major play from any of them as yet is a reflection on the fact that art is not a self-indulgence but a discipline. Tom Eyen is another matter because his personal flair of combining contemporary techniques of fragmentation with popular themes would have made him emerge anywhere—perhaps not in the same form, but with just as much agility.

Although the counterculture has made no important contribution in itself, the influence of its abandon has been felt by all those in the performing arts who want to keep up. Now that the underground theater has surfaced and attracted commercial eyes, Off Off Broadway has difficulty in maintaining its position as a testing ground for fledgling talents to try their wings—the original objective that put the Movement on the side of the angels (no pun intended).